THE PRINCETON REVIEW

LAW SCHOOL COMPANION

THE PRINCETON REVIEW

LAW SCHOOL COMPANION

The Ultimate Guide to Excelling in Law School and Launching Your Career

PAUL M. LISNEK
STEVEN I. FRIEDLAND
CHRIS M. SALAMONE

Random House, Inc.
New York

Dedications

For Mom and Dad, the source of my every accomplishment, and for the future lawyers in my life: David, Michael, and Danielle Lisnek. May you grow up to be everything beautiful that life has to offer. With love—

PML

To my family for always being there, in both good times and bad.

SIF

For my father and best friend, Anthony. For his wisdom, guidance, and unconditional love, trust, and dedication, and in memory of my beloved mother, Rita, who is my constant source of inspiration.

CMS

ISBN 0-679-76150-0

Manufactured in the United States of America on recycled paper

9 8 7 6 5 4 3

Acknowledgments

When we went through law school, it never occurred to us that we would one day write a book on how to succeed there. But years after having experienced law school, we realized that it is possible and necessary to let future lawyers know about what awaits them. The good, the bad, and the fearsome are all part of the law school process; but with a bit of reflection, preparation, and humor, we trust our readers will be able to look back upon their law school years fondly.

We must extend our hearty thanks to some of those who helped bring this book to creation. Thanks to the faculties and administrators of the law schools we attended. To our colleagues at the University of Illinois, Harvard University Law School, and Nova Law Center— accept our deep gratitude for giving us each sound legal training. We have dedicated our own careers to the education of others and are honored to be part of the same tradition to which you belong.

We gratefully acknowledge those people and organizations without whose assistance and support this book would not have been possible. To Professor Michael J. Kaufman, who spent his "off time" at our summer program assisting in the writing and editing of the book. His insight, dedication, and assistance was crucial. To Gary Gassman and Sue Gordon for their invaluable research contributions and for dedicating so much of their time when it was already so precious. To Meredith Frimpter for editing assistance and a keen eye when ours were no longer open. To Eve Brensike for her Daytona 500-style driving, which ensured our meeting all FedEx deadlines. And we extend special appreciation to Donna Kasmer, for offering "on-the-spot" computer assistance to a group of Neanderthals.

To Anthony C. Salamone, administrator of the National Institute for Legal Education, whose undying enthusiasm and constant dedication have long inspired us all. No one person has helped to fulfill NILE's educational mission more profoundly than he.

The NILE administrative team worked non-stop to insure that the office continued to run while we devoted our time to this project. Jessica Orloff, Deanna Betancourt, Lezlie Larson, Anne Brody, Richard Sexton, Steve Pearson, Inez Mede—we thank you for your energy, spirit, and friendship.

To John Katzman and the Princeton Review team, whose hard work made this book a reality.

The heart of the book came from the wisdom we've gleaned from our colleagues at NILE. As the institute has grown, the names have become too numerous to mention, but we do want to express our appreciation to the professors who were there during the formative years: Professors Michael Flynn, Anita Stuppler, Joseph Chaney, Mike Mosca, John Moye, Debra Young, Joe Daly, K. Byron McCoy, Celia Taylor, Andrew Kramer, and Kevin Drumm.

To our students, for their unforgettable enthusiasm, especially those who have returned year after year to meet new students and share their insights with them. Tim Powers (Tulane), David Weizer (George Washington), Julie Steed (Louisiana State University), Jonathan Willan (Harvard), Brian O'Driscall (George Washington), Susan Pupo (Georgetown University), Joe Clark (Harvard), and many others continue to work with us and support our educational mission. Special thanks goes to Nicole Duda, who joined us for the very first program in 1989, worked diligently for the organization for many years, and is our good friend to this day.

Finally, to our families and friends, whose support, encouragement, and faith have been endlessly inspiring.

Paul M. Lisnek
Steven I. Friedland
Chris M. Salamone

Contents

Preface

Your decision to attend law school will certainly be one of the most important and perhaps difficult ones you ever make. A career in law is a commitment to a noble profession that requires stamina, sacrifice, and perseverance. The rewards are well worth the investment if you seek a future devoted to working for justice and resolving disputes between people. We hope you will approach that commitment with dedication and professionalism. If you do, the law will welcome you with open arms.

Over the years, many a law school dean has said something like the following as part of the welcoming speech to newly enrolled students: "Look to your left and look to your right, by the end of your law school career one of the three of you will no longer be with us." While this is certainly a scary scenario, and may statistically still occur in some law schools, the reality is that if you are dedicated and follow the tips and suggestions we offer in this book, you will most likely make it through law school.

The question of how successful you will be remains, however, and is more interesting than it may first appear. If you are like most people who attend law school, you have always been a leader in class. But, in law school, virtually every student in your 1L (first year) class will likely have undergraduate grades and LSAT scores similar to yours, and for the most part will be just as motivated and determined as you are to succeed in law school. Yet, by definition, some students will be at the top of the class, others will be somewhere in the middle, and others will be at the bottom. So, what will make the difference? How can you earn and keep a place in the upper part of the class? Certainly, hard work and dedication help, but these alone are not enough. The students who do well in the first year of law school are the ones who manage to grasp what is known as the law school "process." Unlike anything you have studied before, the road through law school is one traveled only by people who are willing to have their thought processes shifted, their stubbornness exploded, and their every position challenged. That is the lure of the law; it is the art of the profession. You don't get it from books, you can't get it from movies. It comes only from experience, preparation, and commitment. Give us the chance to walk you through the process, and it will all make much more sense when you get there.

This book is intended to take you "inside law school." It will provide you with insights into the law school experience, as well as with strategies and techniques to help you navigate the often confusing and intimidating maze known as "1L." If followed, the principles, strategies, and tips in this book will help you be a much more effective law student. Our reflections are meant to pave the way for your success. By demystifying the process, you will be better prepared for the experience. By believing in yourself, you will succeed. Work hard, work smart, and enjoy the journey. Can't wait? Read on . . .

Paul M. Lisnek
Steven I. Friedland
Chris M. Salamone

CHAPTER 1

So You're Going to Law School

Even the word "excitement" probably doesn't quite capture how you feel as you ready yourself for law school. Your life is about to change dramatically. You may, for example, be journeying to another state to begin your legal education, which is a big move in itself. But even if you are staying at home and attending a local school, you can expect your daily routine and habits to undergo major changes. Late risers may find themselves up with the sun to get in a few more hours of study; and those who used to go to bed early may find themselves becoming familiar with late-night sessions they have never had to bother with before. Adjustment, commitment, and perseverance: we use these words over and over because they will become your mantra for success. Flexibility is the essence of a legal mind: a good lawyer is one who can see all sides of an argument as well as the truth which seems to elude everyone else. This is what you are aiming for. Cases, holdings, rules of law, and briefs: all these terms will become familiar to you in only a few weeks.

> *"Law school is a long, arduous, lonely process no matter where you go. But if you really want to be a lawyer, there is no greater reward."*
> —2L, University of Connecticut

But before you take on the challenge of a lifetime, you should be sure you have all you need to begin law school. We recognize that what follows may seem simplistic, but some things are worth saying over: if you take the time to get your house in order before beginning law school, it will make the transition that much easier. In law school, anything that eases your mind is worth doing.

THE BARE NECESSITIES: HOUSING, TRANSPORTATION, AND OTHER PRACTICALITIES

Housing

Living near the law school you attend will obviously be helpful, especially in your first year. Law school is demanding, and time is an important commodity. Long commutes take up valuable time that could be better spent studying, writing, or even relaxing. So, first up, note that it may be worth spending a little more money in order to save time, download stress, and have easy access to classes and the school's library.

One option is to live on campus. If you are considering doing so, you will need to work out whether the convenience and monetary savings outweigh potential drawbacks such as limited space and living in an environment with students who may or may not have the same work ethic or habits as you. This type of living situation can create, rather than relieve, anxiety, depending on the people with whom you live.

Finding a place to live in a new city is usually time consuming, difficult, and even a little scary. School admissions offices are generally pretty helpful when it comes to finding housing for new students; bear in mind, however, that such housing may not be in the nicest or most interesting parts of a city, and that housing in the heart of metropolitan areas is often very expensive. If you have friends in your new city, ask them for advice on housing matters: where to live, what you can expect to pay, which are the best rental agencies, and so forth. In addition, call the Better Business Bureau or find a phone book or business listing which lists apartment-rental offices. Check around to get their consensus on the nicest and most financially reasonable areas in which to live as well. If you must live far away from school, try to use your commuting time productively. Listening to audiotapes, or car pooling so you can discuss your work with other students, are two ways you can utilize your traveling time efficiently.

Another housing issue is whether or not to live with other people. Just about all students are concerned about money, or to be precise, the lack thereof. As a result, many students have roommates in order to defray expenses. Living with other students can be very rewarding, particularly if friendships develop. As we said above, however, problematic roommates can certainly have an adverse impact on your concentration and overall performance. If you decide to live with other people, screen them carefully. Consider also whether your roommates should include other law students. This may or may not work to your advantage—keep in mind that first-year law students are no treat to live with!

Transportation

You may recall the Steve Martin and John Candy movie, *Planes, Trains, and Automobiles*, in which the famed duo encounter every possible obstacle on their way home for the holidays. See this hilarious movie (it makes for a great study break), but avoid the experience yourself by insuring you have a safe and reliable form of transportation available to you wherever you live. If you live within walking distance of the school, you probably won't need a car. In cities with good public transportation systems, buses and trains will probably get you where you need to go. But studying law is rigorous, and occasionally you may want to get away for a weekend (books do travel and a little reading on a quiet lake or beachfront has a lot going for it!). If you do opt to have a car, make sure you buy one that is safe and reliable. An older or very cheap car may prove to be more trouble than it's worth; you don't want to wind up spending all your valuable study time at the neighborhood mechanic.

Diet and Exercise

In the first year of law school, many students give up or change their eating habits and exercise routines. Their idea of healthy eating becomes coffee with NutraSweet, pizza (double, not triple cheese), and low-fat frozen yogurt. Not only that, but one's former rigorous daily exercise routine is somehow transformed into the path between the library and the vending machine in the student lounge. Even though the workload may seem insurmountable and you will be inclined to give up exercising and eating right . . . don't do it!

The first year of law school is difficult; it is high pressure and high stress. Maintaining a healthy diet and a regular exercise routine will help reduce anxiety and keep you feeling alert, energetic, and better about yourself. There are no extra points in law school for the people with the darkest circles or deepest bags under their eyes. Do it right. Your parents' advice about eating your vegetables, getting enough sleep, and exercising two or three times a week will help keep your mind and body healthy.

"I always make sure that I work out, no matter what! Nothing is worth my own healthy mind and body . . . nothing!"

—1L, Stanford

WHO ARE YOUR CLASSMATES?

Is there a law school "type"? Certainly, there are plenty of myths about who attends law school. Maybe you spent a weekend at your Uncle Bernie's, where you overheard cousin Vinnie say one of the following:

Myth #1: *"She argues so much! She was born to be a lawyer!"*

Myth #2: *"His whole family is in law; it's in his blood."*

Myth #3: *"She can't be in law school; she was an arts major."*

While some people do indeed seem destined for law school from an early age, there is of course no particular pedigree or background required for a career in the law. Although incoming students may be under the impression that a certain persona, background, or college major is particularly suited to a legal career, this is not in fact the case. The following two students are enrolled and performing successfully in law school:

Student #1: My undergraduate degree is in psychology and music. Prior to law school, I worked in the real estate division of a bank and successfully completed an M.B.A. program.

—Georgia State University, Atlanta

Student #2:   I received a master's degree from NYU in music composition; wrote, produced, and directed a rock opera, and co-founded a not-for-profit theater company.

—New York University, New York

"Good lawyers and advisers are not library hermits and the school and students realize that. I like law school better than undergrad—how many schools do you hear that at?"

—1L, University of Virginia

So, during the orientation programs run by many law schools, the admissions director will often proudly announce to the assembled newcomers that the class is both diverse and talented. You will discover that around half the class has gone straight through college directly to law school, while the others have pursued sometimes dull, sometimes fascinating, careers before plunging into their legal training. As we mentioned earlier, you will also discover that over 90 percent of your colleagues did as well as you in college. In the best law schools in the country, this fact means that some 90 percent of the incoming students were in the top 10 percent of their undergraduate class. Intimidating? Sure. Competitive? You bet.

You might perceive the admissions director's proud description of the incoming law students in one of two ways. You may share the admissions director's pride in the class, be flattered to be among such qualified students, and feel that the law school club is a good one. On the other hand, you may find the admissions director's well-intentioned efforts to engage class pride extremely intimidating.

The fact that more than 90 percent of the incoming law students performed at the top of their college class also means that 90 percent of those students will do worse in law school than they did in college. Similarly, the fact that the students are diverse and talented may make those who have gone directly from college to law school feel that they lack experience and maturity. By the same token, those students who have been away from formal education for a number of years may feel that their absence from disciplined study and educational testing will place them at a competitive disadvantage. While such anxieties are real, there is no evidence to suggest that one "type" of law student does better than another. Nor is it possible to create a legitimate typology of law students—they are all different. Rather than being intimidated by the background of other students, you should attempt to embrace the differences and welcome the opportunity to learn from them.

FIRST-DAY FEARS

The thought of going to law school probably fills you with excitement, fear, and frantic anticipation simultaneously. Relax—you've earned your passage into law school and you don't have to be a genius to succeed there. As we've said, it takes commitment, perseverance, and flexibility—qualities you will develop throughout the law, school process. Many lawyers say that the most important quality of a law student is that she or he is prepared for the experience. This makes good sense. Would you run a marathon without training for it? Did you take the LSAT exam without doing any preparation? Of course not.

Many famous and successful people began their careers with a law degree. F. Lee Bailey, Melvin Belli, the President of the United States and his wife, and every judge and lawyer ever to practice law has experienced the process that awaits you. It's ritual, tradition . . . call it what you will. The bottom line is that you can't avoid it. As the old saying goes, ". . . This too shall pass . . . ," and we have every confidence that you will, too.

"The tough part is getting admitted; once you're in, it's a piece of cake."

—*3L, Stanford*

I'M READY TO SUCCEED IN LAW SCHOOL

The Success Factors

In real estate, the most important factor is location. In law, the most important factor might very well be perspective. What will the practice of law mean to you? Will it be your way of life, or will it weigh on your life? Does the art of law imitate life, or is the lawyer's life really an art? You may find yourself pondering such questions as your mind drifts away from those case notes you should be reading for your next class. Here are some thoughts to allay your concerns.

Success Factor #1:   Be Committed to Law School
Law school requires your commitment and dedication. Make the decision to get as much out of law school as it can offer. Law school and lawyering is challenging, exciting, and can even be fun. Take the task seriously, and put in every reasonable effort during your school years. But, above all, keep your dedication to law school in balance with the rest of your life; integrate both in a healthy and meaningful manner.

Success Factor #2:   Keeping Your Objectives in Mind
Most law school students aim to become lawyers and to have long and fulfilling careers in the legal profession. While many misconceptions persist about what lawyers do, due largely to how their role is defined by popular culture, in reality there are many varied career choices available to people who hold law degrees. Lawyers are counselors, interviewers, defenders, proponents, negotiators, advocates, and much more.

Success Factor #3:   Job versus Career
While a person may spend as much time on the job as off it, the time spent at work may not always be overly satisfying. We all know the old adage, "There is a reason why they call it work." It goes without saying that the situation is alleviated if one feels some passion for what one does for a living. Those with a passion often put all they have into their jobs, and can enjoy their work for many, many years.

Many attorneys have a passion for their work, whether it be prosecuting alleged criminals, defending people on death row, or representing the local shoe store or mega corporation. As you proceed through law school, carefully consider which path of the law you wish to practice. What could you feel passionate about for a long time?

Remember Why You're There

Use your passion as inspiration as you proceed through your law school education. It could be something like one of the following:

"I am drawn to issues of gender, race, and ethnicity in the law."

"As a musician, I am interested in copyright law; as a union negotiator, I am interested in labor issues, etc."

"I want to be in the courtroom."

"As a small business owner, I am interested in the tax consequences of business decisions."

"I have been fascinated by the law and lawyering for many years and think I'll enjoy being a lawyer."

"Having been thrust into the legal system through a divorce, my current job with the union, of being victimized in a crime or tort, etc., I want to help others avoid the pitfalls I have experienced."

"I want to work for myself and assist others in understanding their legal rights and obligations."

"I want to assist businesses by providing legal advice."

"I want to help people enforce their rights, protect the environment, safeguard animals from abuse."

"The law provides an intellectually challenging and interesting career."

Student comments

So what do current law students have to say about their decision to attend law school? Here are some of their comments:

"I came to quench my thirst for knowledge and to explore my love of the law. After taking some constitutional law courses in college, I finally found a passion that no other profession has matched."

"As a former paralegal, I was exposed to the day-to-day practice of law and wanted to learn the substance behind the work I was doing."

"I knew that law school wouldn't really be like they show it on television. But I have always been fascinated by watching L.A. Law, Law and Order, *and even* Perry Mason *reruns. Movies like* The Paper Chase *led me to think that I had to experience this process for myself. And I am real glad I have. It's sort of fun."*

DEMISTIFYING THE PROFESSION—
WHAT LAWYERS REALLY DO

Lawyering is often very difficult—-there are difficult bosses, difficult clients, and certainly difficult legal issues. Lawyering is not always about winning or doing justice, and it can involve working long hours under stressful conditions. This is not to say that lawyering is not stimulating, challenging, or rewarding. It can be all these things and more. However, future lawyers should embark on their law school careers with their eyes open.

What lawyers do on a daily basis depends in large part on the nature of their practice. Business attorneys provide counsel to many types of businesses. This includes providing their clients with information regarding the legal ramifications of their proposed business transactions, or representing them after a venture has gone awry and resulted in litigation. These attorneys also assist with acquisitions, mergers, contracts, and other business matters. Real estate attorneys deal with the transfer of real property and disputes about the rights in such property. Environmental attorneys seek redress when environmental regulations have been violated and engage in land-use planning and obtaining the permits necessary to be in compliance with the law. Trial lawyers spend a considerable amount of their time in court, trying cases and participating in hearings and other matters pertaining to litigation. They also spend many hours preparing cases, interviewing witnesses, negotiating with other counsel, and the like. Family lawyers represent individuals involved in family disputes such as divorce, child custody, abuse, abandonment, and neglect. Legal representation may involve mediation, arbitration, and court hearings. Clients, going through difficult times, may range from the extremely grateful to the extremely distraught.

The daily life of an attorney also depends heavily on the nature of the company, firm, or organization for which he or she works.

Some attorneys choose to work with other lawyers in private law firms, while others are sole practitioners, working alone. Still others act as "in-house" counsel, within the legal department of a business or enterprise. In addition, there are government attorneys who work for the local, state, or federal government on various matters, from litigation (prosecutors and public defenders, for example) to the business of governing (the State Department's Office of Legal Counsel, or the County Attorney's Office representing a local community).

Depending on the type of practice, an attorney may spend a considerable amount of time each day doing legal research in the law library, talking on the phone with clients or opposing counsel, traveling and participating in litigation matters such as depositions, or arguing in court in various proceedings. Some lawyers combine these activities, while others focus on only a few of them.

Lawyers in Action

Probably the best way to understand what lawyers do is to observe them in action. This means finding an attorney, perhaps a friend or someone recommended by a legal referral service, whom you can "shadow" for a day or part of a day. You may see, for example, the lawyer begin work at 8:00 a.m. in the office, participate in a 9:00 a.m. deposition (i.e., a specialized interview involving the direct and cross-examination of a witness), conduct a meeting with a prospective client at 11:30 a.m., engage in a conference call with opposing counsel at 1:30 p.m., and meet a business client at the office at 4:00 p.m. Spending time with an attorney in this way offers terrific first-hand information about what lawyering is like. Such a "test drive" may provide important and useful information to you in your future career decisions.

Exercise #1: Looking ahead

While in law school, you can maintain your perspective by keeping in mind where you are headed after school. To assist in this process, write out answers to the following questions.

1. How do you see your future? What do you see yourself doing in five years? Ten years? Fifteen years?

2. What qualities in life are important to you? What are your strengths and weaknesses?

3. If you had not decided to attend law school, what career path would you most likely have chosen? Why?

4. Rank and consider the importance of the following factors as you go through law school:

   a. Intellectual challenge
   b. Emotional rewards
   c. Particular motivation for each career path
   d. Financial rewards
   e. Impact on family life and relationship with friends
   f. Long-term job satisfaction, i.e., twenty years or more
   g. What you hope to accomplish in your career

CHAPTER 2

Before You Begin

PREPARING FOR THE FIRST YEAR:
THE SUMMER BEFORE LAW SCHOOL

The summer before you begin law school is a monumental one. You'll have a lot to do in order to prepare yourself for law school, and it will probably be the last true vacation you'll have for a while. So, what can you do to get yourself in shape for law school?

Friends and Family

First of all, we encourage you to surround yourself with a circle of friends, including other law students and attorneys, who can support you and provide some insights into the law school experience, what you can expect and what will be expected of you. While these people will probably give you invaluable advice, do keep in mind that everyone handles the stress and workload differently. Although others can tell you what law school was like for them, no one can tell you what it will be like for you. Keep their thoughts and comments in perspective.

Books for Summer Reading

Many law schools advise newly admitted students to read about the law or a particular legal case before school begins. Some recommended books concern the law school experience, some concern the philosophy of law (jurisprudence), and some are about influential lawyers and judges (such as Oliver Wendell Holmes, Jr.). Learning about legal education and what law school will entail in general terms is certainly a good place to start, since it helps break down some of the mystique which surrounds the first year of law school. You might consider reading one or two of the following books before you begin your studies.

1. *One L*, Scott Turow.

2. *The Common Law*, Oliver Wendell Holmes, Jr.

3. *Simple Justice: The History of Brown vs. Board of Education*, R. Kluger. Combines history, sociology, and law in its examination of the 1954 Supreme Court decision which declared school segregation unconstitutional. It looks at the Court's deliberations and workings in deciding one of this country's most prominent and important cases.

4. *The Brethren*, B. Woodward & S. Armstrong. Created controversy upon publication for its analysis of the Burger Court's collegial decision making.

5. *Miracle at Philadelphia*, C. D. Bowen. Examines the history of the 1787 Constitutional Convention.

6. *The Buffalo Creek Disaster*, G. Stern. Graphically details events surrounding the 1972 flooding of twenty to thirty communities in the Buffalo Creek valley when a coal company's dam collapsed. It describes the nature of attorneys and the litigation process through the eyes of the Buffalo Creek plaintiffs' attorney.

Find a Law-Related Job?

Although it sounds like a great idea, finding a law-related job before beginning law school may not actually be of much value to you. Obtaining a clerkship or research position before you've completed even a semester of law school may be nearly impossible anyway, and even if you do so, working for a law firm or legal organization as a lower-level employee will provide you with virtually no experience that will be helpful in law school. Neither will it provide you with references that will make you a more desirable employee than anyone else. In addition, you may find the tasks and material quite confusing, so the experience may only serve to sour your outlook on law school. For all these reasons, it is advisable to wait until you have completed at least one semester of law school before attempting to obtain work in the legal field.

Additional College Classes

Some people recommend taking a course or two the summer before law school begins. If you decide to do so, classes in writing and communications will be the most beneficial. Few people seem to realize how much writing is required in law school or how much grade emphasis is placed on one's ability to write well. Possessing superior communications skills is advantageous to law students and lawyers in obvious ways. In fact, they are a must!

Visit the Law School and Attend A Class

In addition to hearing about law school from your friends and acquaintances, as a future student you may sit in on classes and visit law school campuses. Visiting classes can be arranged through the school's admissions office and gives you the opportunity to see first-hand how classes are conducted. And of course the good news is that as a visitor the odds are high that you won't be called on to answer any questions!

Of course, as a passive observer, neither will you experience the intensity, stress, and frustration of the classroom experience or the hours of preparation required for each class. It is these additional factors that can make the first year of law school so difficult.

Most law schools offer formal tours of the school which include looking over the physical facilities and sitting in on a class. Some schools also offer a more extensive "Dean's Coffee" or similar type of formal introductory session for applicants as well. These sessions are usually held at night or on weekends a few times each year. The dean, faculty members, members of the admissions committee or admissions office, or a combination of the above, will lead the discussion, which typically centers on what life is like at the school, and often includes a question-and-answer session. All this can be very valuable to you. You may even be treated to a mock class led by a faculty member in which applicants—and sometimes spouses, family members, and friends—can participate.

Your visit to a school need not be a formal one you have arranged with a school official. You may prefer simply to hang out in the student lounge area; most law students are more than willing to talk with you about their school and their experiences there. Note whether the students you meet are in their first, second, or third year, since that will often color their view of the educational process. Don't be surprised if second- or third-year students are a little more judgmental.

Law School Orientation Program

Many law schools now run special orientation programs for incoming first-year students. These can last from several hours to several days. Orientation programs often include speeches and presentations by various members of the law school administration and law school organizations, such as law review, legal fraternities, etc., as well as by students. Some programs may also include sample law school classes. The atmosphere is generally friendly and unintimidating.

Law School Prep Program

One way you can go much further than spectating is by taking a preparatory program which simulates the first-year law school experience by immersing students in a realistic law school environment. Since 1989, the motto "Real Professors—Real Classes—Real Law School" has come to symbolize the National Institute for Legal Education's summer and winter law school prep programs. These programs offer substantive law classes, strategies for succeeding in class and on exams, and help ease anxiety by demystifying the law school aura. NILE holds its intensive law school prep programs each summer and in January over the winter break. Students are taught each course in the first-year law school curriculum by distinguished professors who use casebooks and the famous "Socratic method" to create a realistic law school environment. For more information about NILE's Law School Prep Program, or to speak with former program students who are now in law school, call (800) FYI-NILE.

Student comments

This is what students had to say when asked what they did to prepare themselves for law school:

> *"I talked to practicing attorneys to determine what types of law I might be interested in."*

"I visited a law school as a prospective student, observed classes, and talked to students."

"I read One L *and visited my brother at law school."*

"I spent a lot of time talking to my mother and my father who are both attorneys. We discussed the pros and cons. I also visited a few campuses."

"I attended a NILE Law School Prep Program. It was absolutely invaluable. It provided a crucial foundation in preparation for law school and definitely gave me an advantage in the first year. I strongly recommend it."

THE BUCKS START HERE

Going to law school must be an affordable endeavor for you, or you must be willing to accept the significant debt that you will incur. Can you afford tuition, room and board, relocation, books, and other necessary expenses? Secondary financial considerations may also apply, such as the cost of giving up an income, the price of reducing your current lifestyle, and the pressures and other factors involved in having loans and relocating your assets. You need to evaluate all such costs well in advance. If you have not thought about your financial situation before summer arrives, you may run into trouble. Certainly, loan money disbursements will be late, even months into the fall semester, if you have not applied in the spring.

Once you have worked out a realistic estimate of how much money you will need, start gathering your resources from the schools to which you apply, from libraries, your college pre-law advisor, and your bank. Each institution will have information on student loans, including application procedures, dates, current intrest rates, and perhaps even various financial plans. Scholarship information may be obtained from some of the same sources.

"Columbia is a great law school for those who chew nails for breakfast, want to work for a prestigious law firm, and have no fear of massive debt. If you have a problem with that, save your money."

—2L Columbia

Loans

Consulting with the law school's financial planning office is a good place to start regarding tuition scholarships and loan programs. Other potential sources of help and advice are your family and friends, who may be willing to assist not only with loans, but also with other needs such as room and board.

Schools and the government evaluate loan requirements by taking into account the cost of attending a particular school, less family contributions and other types of financial aid to which you may be entitled. Even if you are dependent on your parents, loans may still be available if you do not live at home during law school. If you are not dependent on your parents, or have a family of your own, financial assistance may be available depending on expected changes in your financial situation. For example, there may be a considerable loss of income if you need to quit a job in order to attend law school. Since government loan policies are often subject to change, make sure you obtain current information. Such information is available from: The Federal Student Aid Information Center, Post Office Box 84, Washington, DC 20044.

Information may also be available at schools, public libraries, and participating lending institutions. One of the better sources is the Law School Admissions Services, Box 2000, Newtown, Pennsylvania, 18940-0998. The LSAS has information on various loan programs.

Other Forms of Financial Assistance

Financial aid is also available in the form of scholarships, which do not have to be repaid, as well as work-study programs which allow the student to work on campus for an hourly rate. Often, a school will allot a student on work-study a particular sum of money during the course of the semester.

Some schools also have special research fellowships or grants for faculty members which can be used for student research assistants. This is generally available for second- and third-year students only, but may be available to first-years as well. This information can be obtained by calling the law school.

Students who earn a position on their school's law review or moot court board often receive tuition reimbursement or credit for their participation. While such opportunities are available to only a few students and exist only at a limited number of schools, they may be worth checking out. You may be one of the lucky few!

Summer Work

Apart from loans and scholarships, many students of course work each summer, both inside and outside the legal profession, in order to make money to help them through the next year. Likewise, some students work the twenty hours a week allowed by the American Bar Association during their second and third years in school.

A Note on Fees

Finally, it is important to note that tuition and fees are not necessarily related to either the quality of the education a person receives at an institution or its reputation. Private schools will generally cost considerably more than public schools, but there is no denying that every law school is an expensive proposition. Go in with your eyes and your pocketbook open. You may or may not make up the debt quickly upon graduation; however you will never regret having completed a law school education.

CHAPTER 3

Succeeding in the First Year

THE LAW SCHOOL EXPERIENCE: A THREE-YEAR OVERVIEW

It's your first day of law school. You enter your first class and you and the other students sit quietly, and nervously, in your seats. The door opens and the professor walks briskly to the front of the room. She carries a seating chart under her right arm and a casebook in her left hand. She approaches the podium, places the seating chart on it, opens the book to page one, and stares ferociously down at the chart. You and your classmates fidget. You're expecting words of welcome, a few words of encouragement, and the opening lecture, which will probably be an introduction to the course. The professor speaks: "The facts of *Palsgraf v. Long Island Railroad* ... Ms. . . ." Oh my goodness, is she about to call on me? Please, no! I didn't read the case . . . I'm not ready! You look down, hoping the professor doesn't spot you. Your heart beats hard, and a lump rises in your throat . . .

Relax. This is just a book. You're not in law school yet. Had this been an actual class, though, you might have been in for a less-than-pleasant experience. But read on. This chapter is about, among other things, preparing yourself for the moment. The fact is, you just don't need to experience the fear and anxiety that many have felt before you. There is a common phrase you will hear around law school and may well have heard already: the first year, they (the law professors) scare you to death; the second year, they work you to death; the third year, they bore you to death. Nothing else you ever hear will be closer to the truth.

During your first year at law school, you'll probably be a bit anxious or frightened. Some professors prey on this fear. Reading assignments may be confusing, and classroom interrogations may only add to your anxiety. In college, you became used to professors who gave lectures, who offered compliments for insightful comments, and who were patient and helpful when less-than-astute remarks were made. All in all, we have to tell you, this type of positive experience will not be repeated in law school. In law school, each question is followed by another question, no answer seems to be correct, and each answer is met with another question. Scary? You bet. That's why, in the first year, it's said, "they scare you to death." But you will get used to it, and after a while you'll begin to understand the purposes of the "classroom game."

By the time the second year rolls around, you'll think you've got it down. You made it through the first year; you're ready to handle anything. But here's the deal, professors now treat you as though you have no other class except theirs, piling on the work with no concern about whether you have a job on the side, or whether you have a wedding to attend in another state, or whether you are ill. Excuses are not acceptable. You are expected to meet all your obligations. Diligence and determination are the keys to surviving the second year. Hence, in the second year, it's said, "they work you to death."

Finally, you reach the third year. Psychologically, you're ready to get out into the real world and, if you're like most students, you've chosen to remain working at your summer job during the school year. After all, this may become your permanent job if the firm or lawyer needs you, and you have debts and loans to pay off. In your third year, you may find you have less time for school; indeed, "they are boring you to death." You have learned the tricks of the trade, the process of thinking like a lawyer. The workload is less burdensome, and you consider starting a petition to make law school a two-year curriculum. You're tired of being in school. You're approaching the light at the end of the tunnel.

DEFINING SUCCESS IN LAW SCHOOL

Before you can succeed in law school, it's important to define exactly what this means. To most people, success is determined by grades, honors (e.g., becoming a member of the law review or moot court), and employment. Yet many people define success in other ways, incorporating family, friends, effort, and integrity into their definition. How you approach law school depends on how you define success.

Exercise #2: What is success?

State briefly how would you define success in law school, giving reasons for your answer.

_____

_____

THE REALITY OF LAW SCHOOL

The differences between law school and college are significant enough to require a totally new adjustment period, as we mentioned in the first chapter of this book. These differences range from the way classes are organized to the focuses of the learning process, to the relationships between peers. While the law school experience obviously differs from school to school and from one person to another, there are some general things that law school definitely is not:

- Lectures
- Lawyering practice
- A breeze
- A place without friends
- For geniuses only
- Something you can understand without experience
- Mere memorization of rules and principles to be repeated on examinations

Exercise #3: What is law school like?

For each of the following questions, circle the best answer and give a brief explanation for your choice.

1. **True/False** Law teachers begin class with an explanation of the material and what it means. They then offer their views as to what the significance of the case is and how it should have been decided. Finally, they ask for questions.

   _____

   _____

2. **True/False** In law school, students study different types of lawyering, such as how to do real-estate closing, how to handle child-custody proceedings, and how to perform mergers and acquisitions.

   _____

   _____

3. Of the following, which student is most likely to receive the highest grade in class:

   a. the person who speaks the most times during class discussion
   b. the person who has the longest outline
   c. the person whom the professor likes the most
   d. the quiet person on your left who never says a word in class but who can spot, evaluate, and analyze issues extremely well

   _____

   _____

4. If a student either fails to attend class regularly or regularly shows up unprepared, a law professor is most likely to:

   a. not care at all
   b. applaud the student if she or he receives a good grade on the examination anyway
   c. lower the student's grade, reprimand the student, or request that the student prepare in the future
   d. chaperon the student to the final examination

   _____

   _____

5. Law students are generally evaluated on a minimum of:

   a. three quizzes and a final examination
   b. a midterm and a final examination
   c. a final examination
   d. three writing courses and a clinical program before graduation

   _____

   _____

6. At least 20 percent of the first-year class:

   a. flunks out
   b. cries in class
   c. believes at one time or another that they are not smart enough to attend law school
   d. will be admitted to an honors track in law school

   _____

   _____

7. Most law students:

   a. cannot be trusted with anything
   b. will cheat or steal during their first year
   c. have experienced the Socratic method at length in college
   d. will receive lower grades than they expect

   _____

   _____

Answers

1. False. Law teachers ask a series of questions, which, by inference, suggests how to analyze and evaluate the subject matter. It is left solely to students to create a framework of analysis and strategies for dealing with the material. Law teachers approach the material indirectly and implicitly.

2. False. Lawyering activities are not usually taught in law school. Most of the time in school is spent learning legal rules and principles and how to think about them. The various activities regularly engaged in by a lawyer, such as real-estate closing, are learned after a student graduates and enters his or her area of practice.

3. d. There may be little correlation between those who speak often in class and those who perform well on examinations. The skill of oral presentation does not necessarily correspond to the skill of writing an examination under significant time pressure. There are always students who hardly speak in class but who do well on examinations.

4. c. The American Bar Association requires class attendance. Your professors make their own policies. Some permit a certain number of absences before lowering the final grade, others are not as strict.

5. c. Perhaps the biggest adjustment most law students must make relates to the evaluation process. Unlike college, where several tests or quizzes are commonly used to determine a student's final grade on a course, in law school one final examination per course usually determines the final grade.

6. c. The fact is that law schools and law students are competitive. Almost every student has feelings of inferiority at one time or another, and there is often no positive feedback to alleviate such feelings.

7. d. Most of your fellow law students will have graduated in the top part of their college classes and will be accustomed to earning "A" and "B" grades. In law school, the grading scale is often tougher than in most colleges. For example, a "B" grade will generally place a student near the top of the class.

Exercise #4: Define your terms

New law students sometimes confuse the distinctions between the law, lawyering, and legal education. Write out what you think each of these terms means.

1. The law

   _____

   _____

2. Lawyering

   _____

   _____

3. Legal education

   _____

   _____

4. Compare Law, Lawyering, and Legal education. What are the similarities and the differences?

_____

_____

_____

Answers

1. The law consists of binding rules and principles imposed by society to govern the conduct of its members. There are various sources of law, such as the legislature, judges, administrative bodies, and constitutions or charters.

2. Lawyering involves the practice of law. Generally a lawyer specializes in a particular area of law, such as employment discrimination, adoptions, prosecution, labor law, trademark, and the like. Lawyering involves solving problems, usually how the law applies to specific facts, and persuading others, namely juries and judges, through reason.

3. Legal education is the three-year process by which students learn to think like lawyers. Students learn about a variety of subject areas and legal skills, particularly how to analyze various legal doctrines.

"Efforts are made to make the student's experience fun, but ultimately a student at Wayne will get out of law school what he or she puts into it. No one is going to lead you by the hand, but if you're hard-working and competitive you can get an excellent education."
—1L, Wayne State

TRACKING THE FIRST YEAR OF LAW SCHOOL

If you are like most students, your first year of law school will go something like this:

June-July: Consider attending the National Institute for Legal Education's two-week law school preparation course.

August: Prepare to move to law school, attend orientation, and get ready for some fairly significant lifestyle changes. Get to know your new colleagues. Buy books and other course materials.

September: Get acquainted with your classmates and the in-class methodology. Begin making course outlines; form study groups; ask "Am I briefing cases properly?" Learn to balance your work and play time.

October: Enjoy the challenges presented by the cases. Legal research and writing is constant and demanding. Thoughts like, "Where does all my time go?" and "I need an extra hour or two" crop up frequently.

November: Most students begin to get a bit weary. Reading case #1,000 is not as thrilling as reading case #1. Plan a study schedule for the final exams. Finals loom and serious studying begins around Thanksgiving.

December: Finals, finals, finals. Is there anything else in the world? Afterwards, take a well-deserved break. The wait for grades begins.

January: Grades, grades, grades. Some exult; others become cynical. "But I knew the stuff better than anyone." Or, "It's only the first set of grades, big deal." The moot court brief moves to the forefront.

February: The students finish the moot court brief only to play catch-up with the substantive classes. Start to think about what to do during the summer. Who is already interviewing for jobs and who received what offers?

March: The oral argument. More fun than at first glance. "Should I continue on into the subsequent single elimination competition? And what about the summer? I guess I should start thinking about that."

April: Work on outlines. Is it finals time again? Prepare a study guide.

May: Finals, finals, finals . . . .

June: Summer school? Vacation? Work? Think it through.

August: Here we go again, but you're in control now!

> *"Going to law school is a lot like having your teeth pulled—you know it hurts but you're usually numb from the pain."*
>
> —— *3L, Valparaiso*

THE FIRST-YEAR CURRICULUM

The first-year law school curriculum is generally fixed for students across the country. Most often the first year requires that students take courses in contracts, criminal law, torts, civil procedure, property, constitutional law, legal research and writing, and sometimes professional responsibility.

Contracts

Contracts is perhaps the quintessential first-year law course. It explores a basic societal relationship: the agreement. Contract principles include what is required to form a binding agreement, at what point a breach of that agreement occurs, and what damages are required as a result of a breach.

Criminal Law

Criminal law analyzes the principles of punishment, the prerequisites to making conduct criminal, and the elements of crimes. The jurisprudence of moral blameworthiness is examined, since culpability plays a large role both in determining whether conduct is criminal and the degree to which it will be considered criminal. A person's mental state and the explanation (that is, defense) of why an act has been committed are important in determining whether the act will be considered criminal. As the famous jurist, Oliver Wendell Holmes Jr., once said, "Even a dog can distinguish between being stumbled over and being kicked." Various common-law crimes are considered, with emphasis on criminal homicide, particularly murder and manslaughter.

Torts

This course in some ways parallels criminal law. Both courses discuss the elements of wrongs, including the act, the mental state and causation, and defenses. Unlike criminal law, however, which explores crimes against society, tort law analyzes civil wrongs between private individuals or the government and a private individual. A considerable amount of time in the course is spent on the subject of negligence.

Civil Procedure

This course provides a road map for civil lawsuits, from initiation of a suit until trial. As the course title implies, it focuses on the processes of a lawsuit, particularly some of the limitations on bringing suit. For example, students explore the question of whether the court is the right court to hear the matter, and whether the particular parties to the suit are in the appropriate court. Students also learn about pre-trial and post-trial motions, and, at some schools, learn to draft pleadings.

Property

In a property class, students learn about the rules and principles governing real property (land), including the evolution of property law from feudal times to the present. Also covered are the various interests that exist in private property, from life estates to fee simples, from springing future interests to shifting future interests. In addition, students learn about the law of landlords and tenants and other interests in property, such as easements.

Constitutional Law

In some schools, a course on the rudiments of constitutional law is offered in the first year. This course often focuses on the powers of the federal and state governments to enact laws and the ways in which these powers are divided and separated. Some constitutional law courses also include the rights and limitations on the government, such as due process, equal protection, and freedom of speech. In many schools, various rights, such as the Bill of Rights and the Fourteenth Amendment protections of due process and equal protection, are taught in a separate course (or courses).

Legal Research and Writing

In almost every school, students are required to take a full-year course on legal research and writing. This course is generally allocated fewer credits than other first-year courses, but is just as likely to take up the bulk of students' time and effort. There are several reasons for this. It is probably the only class in which students receive evaluation and feedback before the completion of the first semester and final examinations—the course involves turning in weekly or semi-weekly assignments. Furthermore, there is often more one-to-one interaction in this class, since the class size is generally much smaller than in the substantive courses.

In the first semester of this program, students learn the fundamentals of legal research and writing, which often culminates in writing a memorandum of law requiring both research of the common law and/or statutes and writing. In the second semester, students write a brief, and participate in an oral argument about the case in question.

COURSE MATERIALS

Used versus New Books

Many people recommend that you purchase new books for at least your first semester at law school. This is a very good piece of advice. While new books are more expensive, they are not marred by someone else's highlighting. When a text is already highlighted, people have a tendency to pay more attention to the colored material, and how can you trust the habits of the previous book owner? For all you know, that person may have failed the first year. If saving money needs to be your priority, then, of course, used books are the best way to go, but look for the ones with the fewest marks. If you are forced to buy a heavily highlighted text, be aware of the problems this can cause.

Study guides are items you can always buy used. These materials supplement your study and need not be in perfect shape. They are also expensive, so you'll save money buying them second-hand. Make sure you buy the updated versions, however, otherwise you'll be studying some irrelevant material and will have made a poor investment even though you saved money on the cover price.

The Legal Dictionary

One item you must purchase in your first year is a good legal dictionary. Although it may seem expensive, you will have it for years. A good dictionary is important because language and the use of words make up the cornerstone of both law school and lawyering. Additionally, many legal terms are difficult to figure out simply by inference. It is always wise to have a dictionary on hand.

Legal dictionaries provide more detailed information than you might expect, making them a research tool and study guide as well. For instance, many of the words you will encounter are Latin in origin, and legal dictionaries contain whole sections which teach you about Latin and its pronunciation.

"I have received the best possible legal education here. The best thing, in my opinion, is that I feel I could walk out the door on graduation day and into a courtroom and know exactly what to do."

—— *3L, Campbell*

THE LAW SCHOOL CLASS

How To Do It Right

Taking Notes by Hand

When taking notes in a law school class, make sure you include what the professor asks, not only what appear to be the rules and principles and the way they apply in certain fact contexts. Understanding the professor's perspective is very useful in putting together the pieces of a course. Additionally, what professors ask in class often hints at what they will ask on the final exam. Certainly, writing down the class discussions will help you analyze the situations presented, and by extension will allow you to key into the type of analysis required by the professor, which will probably help you write a better final exam.

Laptops

With the computer age in full force, many students now use laptop computers for taking notes in class. Though initially an expensive investment, they can be very helpful, especially if you type quickly. Typing the class discussion directly into your computer will also save time when you come to do outlines, because the material will already be there for you to edit.

Some schools have modernized classrooms which include computers and the means by which you can connect your own computer directly to the system. Professors often lecture in these labs, providing students with exercises which can be downloaded into their personal computers for review later. All in all, then, purchasing a laptop is definitely worth considering.

Taping Lectures

It is our feeling that taping class is not worth the effort. Your future study schedule is unlikely to permit you to review the tapes anyway. Moreover, you must be sure that you don't just tune out during class in favor of listening to the tapes later.

There is no doubt that tapes would supplement your notes, particularly if the discussion moves very fast. But, again, remember that you may not find the time to listen to them, so never try to use the tapes instead of taking notes.

Abbreviations

Note-taking is a cumbersome process whether or not you use a computer, but there are a few traditionally used abbreviations which make the task much easier. Some of the more common ones are:

Plaintiff: P or π

Defendant: D

Versus: v.

Court: Ct.

Supreme Court: S.Ct., S/C

Appellate Court: App., A/C

District Court: D.Ct., D/C

Respondent: Resp.

Petitioner: Petit.

Chief Judge: C.J.

Concurrence: Conc.

Dissent: Dis.

Reasonable: R'ble

Jurisdiction: -J-

Summary Judgment: SJ

Contract: K

Criminal Code: Cr. Code

Evidence: Ev.

Penal Code: P.C.

Remanded: Rem'd

Affirmed: Aff'd

Appellate Division: App. Div.

Attorney General: Att'y Gen.

Majority of Jurisdictions: Maj.

Minority of Jurisdictions: Min.

Bankruptcy: Bkrtcy

Holding of the Case: H

Issue of the Case: I

Rule of the Case: R

Procedural Posture of the Case: Proc. P

The Classroom Game

At the beginning of this chapter we mentioned one of the peculiarities of the law school education, the "classroom game." We described a situation in which questions are met with more questions, and the search for an "answer" often results in nothing but a dead end. More than this, class notes may make little sense, since you're uncertain of what, if anything, is of value or will help you in preparing for exams. All this can be highly frustrating until you learn the rules of the game.

We said that the classroom game is designed to change the way you think. The aim is to teach you to think like a lawyer, which means being able to take a set of facts (that is, what happened), apply the law to those facts in order to determine what the relevant (that is, legally significant) issues are or what issues are created by those facts, and to form an argument as to why one side or the other should prevail.

The answer to who is right or wrong in a case always seems to depend: it depends on whose perspective you look at it from, that is, who your client is. While you are still in the classroom, it is important that you try to see both sides of an issue and be prepared to defend your position by way of clear, logical analysis.

As part of your law school education you will learn the rules of law, and it is these you will apply to the facts of a case. As a student you will read many cases which were decided and subsequently overturned, or where the professor does not agree with the decision. Each case you read will set forth a rule of law and you will need to understand how the court came to its decision. Each new case will build on the ones which precede it and lead to the ones which follow. This is an important process to grasp because it is also what a lawyer does in her work. A lawyer is faced with an issue which she must distinguish within the law and based on the facts presented. Like a hypothetical in class, the lawyer in practice looks at the facts, then compares them to preceding cases and plans for those which may follow.

The Socratic Method

The primary teaching technique in law school is the Socratic dialogue, whereby the teacher asks one or more students a series of questions without providing answers. Thus, the teacher becomes a source of probing questions, who leaves students an indirect and uncertain trail of what's important and why. Needless to say, this type of classroom methodology can be intimidating and frustrating for students, especially those who are accustomed to guidance and are lost without concrete, definitive answers. Students often have difficulty with the ambiguity of the process and the fact that there appear to be "no answers." Being able to deal with this ambiguity will significantly reduce the discomfort of the first year at law school. Here is an example of how a dialogue might go:

> *Professor: Does a university agree to supervise its students?*
>
> *Student: No, there is no express agreement in Hegel.*
>
> *Professor: Aren't there such expectations if a student lives in a dormitory?*
>
> *Student: Probably not, because again there is no agreement.*

Professor: Wouldn't the provision of room and board equate to what parents provide?

Student: Not exactly, since parents would exercise more control over their children.

Professor: What if the university dorm had a curfew, or a floor supervisor, or a resident assistant? Would that change your answer?

Student: Only if it related to whether a contractual agreement existed.

Professor: Why?

Student: There can be no liability for inaction.

Professor: If the student lived at home, would that change your answer?

Student: Possibly.

Professor: Why? And would it make a difference if the student was not seventeen but eighteen? Why? Could such a minor be presumed to have sufficient maturity not to require supervision? Why?

Student: Well, levels of maturity vary widely and don't exactly depend on age. Further . . .

Not all law professors use the Socratic method (and those who do may apply it in various ways). Some teachers prefer to lecture, work in small discussion groups, or use problem-solving or other simulation exercises. For example, in civil procedure, students may draft a complaint; in contracts there may be a contract negotiation; in criminal law there may be a mock trial to determine whether a person has committed a crime, and in torts a negligence action may be tried before a jury of students.

Legal Reasoning

Legal reasoning, or learning to "think like a lawyer," is the focus of most of the first year of law school. Through the use of reason students learn how to persuade others ethically. While much advocacy outside the legal profession involves emotion and/or force, ethical advocacy favors civility and the use of authority, corroboration, or support to persuade others. Legal reasoning operates from a set of premises or rules, and applies those rules to various factual situations. Conclusions are justified and supported in one of two ways—through precedent or policy.

Precedent generally occurs in the form of common law cases or legislative enactments called statutes. First-year students spend most of their time on case analysis, that is, learning how to interpret cases.

Interpretations of legal rules and principles and the creation of legal rules and principles often depend not on precedent but on policies that transcend the individual case. Public policies include:

1. Morality, which asserts that something is good or bad in and of itself

2. Utility, which argues about efficiency (costs and benefits), deterrence, and gloom and doom (terrible outcomes)

3. Administrability, or whether a workable rule can be devised

4. Competency—whose job is it to decide the issue?

An illustration of how precedent and policy can apply is the question of the appropriateness of the death penalty. Is such a penalty valid?

The following exercises are intended to provide you with an opportunity to practice legal reasoning.

Exercise #5: "Is a lawn mower a driven vehicle?"

1. If you were the judge in the following case, how would you rule and why? Explain your conclusions.

   Facts: Edna Cummings went to a dinner party one Saturday night in June in a small Ohio town. She drank what for her was an unusually large quantity of alcohol at the party—four vodka tonics, two beers, and three Bloody Marys. After being driven home at midnight, she went into her garage and started riding around on her tractor-style lawn mower. Soon, she was zigging and zagging all over her neighbors' nicely manicured lawns, cutting fresh but irregular paths in their grass.

The police arrived after she had begun to ride the lawn mower over neighbor number eight's property.

Edna was arrested and charged with violating Ohio Statute 246.7, "Driving a Vehicle While Intoxicated," a misdemeanor criminal offense for first-time offenders. Edna's lawyer argued that she was not driving a vehicle and that therefore the statute did not apply to her.

_____

_____

_____

_____

_____

_____

_____

2. What is the relevance of each of the following precedents?

   a. *Arbuckle v. State:* An Ohio appeals court held that a drunken pilot could not be prosecuted under the "Driving a Vehicle While Intoxicated" statute. The Court held that an airplane was not a vehicle.

   b. *Bronson v. State:* The Ohio Supreme Court held that a drunken bicyclist could be prosecuted under the statute because it was a vehicle that equated with an automobile, truck, or motorcycle. It was being used in a similar manner and the purpose of the statute was to prohibit such a dangerous use.

_____

_____

_____

Answers

1. Whether Edna is convicted depends on whether she was "driving a vehicle." Her charge of intoxication will probably not become a disputed issue. Whether she was driving a vehicle, in turn, depends on both precedent and policy. If the purpose of the statute is to deter dangerous use of the roads, then Edna is not guilty because she wasn't on a road. If the statute was simply designed to prevent the subject from the use of any motorized vehicle while intoxicated, then she would be guilty. Must a vehicle be motorized? Be designed for use primarily on the road? Be intended to provide transportation?

2a. Whether a tractor-style lawn mower is like an airplane.

2b. Whether a tractor-style lawn mower can be equated with a bicycle and therefore falls within the holding of the case.

Exercise #6: "Ten items or fewer"

1. According to a new United States customs regulation, individuals entering the United States from other countries who carry into the country ten or fewer "items" are entitled to be processed in a special "quick" lane. Duty is paid per item, and it is stated in the regulations that by limiting the number of items carried, inspectors will be able to process people much more rapidly. As an employee of the customs service, you have been asked to define with particularity the definition of "items" and explain your reasoning.

   a. My definition:

   _____

   _____

b. The reasoning behind my definition:

_____

_____

2. You have been asked how to count the following under your definition:

   a. Six pairs of shoes—as six or twelve items?

   _____

   _____

   b. Two six-packs of soda—as two or twelve items?

   _____

   _____

   c. A pack of cigarettes containing twelve cigarettes—one item or twelve?

   _____

   _____

   d. Four cans of tennis balls, each of which holds three balls—as four or twelve items?

   _____

   _____

   e. Twelve apples, placed equally in two open plastic bags—as two or twelve items?

   _____

   _____

Answers

The construction of this rule depends on (a) the function of the item; (b) its packaging; (c) how the goods are traditionally sold; or (d) a combination of these.

    a. Pairs of shoes: Based on function, how shoes are usually sold (in pairs), and the usual packaging of two shoes to a box, six pairs of shoes should count as six items.

    b. Six-packs of soda: If packaged in plastic and sold for one price, this would probably count as two items.

    c. Package of cigarettes: This question is to be contrasted with the six-pack of soda. Whether the cigarettes count as twelve items or one item depends on the significance of a lack of packaging binding them together.

    d. Two cans of tennis balls: This is perhaps an easier question, since most cans of tennis balls are sold as a single entity; certainly the packaging and function also support such a construction.

    e. Apples in two open plastic bags: The placement of the apples in the plastic bags should not be dispositive of how to consider them. If the apples are sold separately, packaged separately, and used separately, then they are likely twelve items. Comparing the apples with the twelve bottles of soda, however, may indicate that the apples are four items, especially if they are all sold at the same price.

Exercise #7: "To live or die In Arizona"

The following information is based on the facts of *Tison v. Arizona, U.S.* Read it through and answer the questions below.

The Supreme Court of the United States has held that the death penalty may be lawfully administered to a person who has committed an aggravated murder, that is, one which is especially heinous or cruel.

Suppose that two boys, ages eighteen and nineteen, have been visiting their father in prison for ten years on a regular basis. Their father, Gary, is serving a prison term of eighteen years for murder. The boys, Raymond and Ricky, love him very much. When he suggests that they break him out of prison, the boys readily agree. The father devises a plan whereby Raymond and Ricky will smuggle several automatic weapons into the prison in a picnic basket. They will tie up the guards at gunpoint, and Gary will be free.

The escape is carried off without a hitch. Within a day of the escape, however, the car breaks down and they flag down a couple with an infant on a remote road. At gunpoint, Gary and the boys force the couple to give up their car. Then, Gary takes the couple and infant to the broken-down car and calmly shoots them all. The boys thought that Gary was going to leave the family there with water, and are taken aback by their father's conduct. The next day, in a shootout with the police, Gary is killed and the boys are captured.

> If convicted, can the boys be lawfully sentenced to death? Should the boys be held responsible for the deaths of the family? Why?

_____

_____

_____

_____

_____

_____

Answer

First up, it should be noted that your ultimate conclusion will not be as important as the analysis you use in reaching it. You must provide support or authority to back up your assertions, in the form of precedent or policy or both. Thus, whether you think the boys should or should not be held liable is secondary to why you think so.

One way to answer this question is to conclude that the boys should be held liable because they created the escape that resulted in the deaths of the couple and the infant. Further, the boys acted in reckless disregard of life by supplying automatic weapons to a convicted murderer. Individuals who act in reckless disregard of human life in such a manner have acted heinously and should be held responsible for Gary's actions.

Another way to respond to this question is to conclude that the boys should not be held liable for their naïve and unflinching love for their father. The boys' love for their father blinded their view of him and the likelihood that he would harm others. While the boys are culpable actors, they should not be held responsible for the actions of their father that they did not anticipate.

Exercise #8: Ethical reasoning

1. Which of the following criminals should be punished the most severely? And the least severely? Ethically persuade a person who has a viewpoint diametrically opposed to yours. What reasons would you use?

Person #1: A local drug dealer who sells small quantities of cocaine on the street.

Person #2: A stockbroker who has embezzled $4 million from her company.

Person #3: A burglar who specializes in home burglaries during the day when no one is at home.

Person #4: A person who was driving drunk at 2 a.m. one morning, but who did not cause an accident.

Person #5: A person who robs people at gunpoint at ATM machines.

Person #6: A person who owns a small business which unlawfully dumps garbage in the woods.

---

2. Sondra and Arnold have been married for seven years. Because they wanted children, although not in the immediate future, they froze five embryos. Recently, the marriage fell apart. During the divorce proceeding, both Sondra and Arnold wanted the embryos. Sondra wanted to destroy them, and Arnold wanted to bring the embryos to term through a surrogate.

What are the policy arguments for and against giving the embryos to Arnold? And to Sondra? What if Sondra wanted to bring the embryos to term and Arnold wanted to destroy them. Would the result be different?

> *"I believe that law school is a great education for anyone, even if there are too many lawyers. It teaches critical thinking, which is important for an individual's growth, as well as that of society. I also believe it makes one more aware of our individual transactions and activities in life, which fosters change for the better. I would never discourage anyone from getting a degree in law, although I might discourage a person from becoming a lawyer."*
>
> —3L, Widener

Class Participation

Students participate in class in one of two ways—by volunteering or by being called upon to answer the professor's questions. Some students love talking in class and readily volunteer; others hate it with a passion and do not contribute unless they have to. Most students, of course, fall somewhere in between these extremes.

The prospect of being called on to speak in class makes many students nervous. This reaction is widespread and entirely natural (one study found that public speaking was more feared by people than death). While being called on may feel like the end of the world to the person being asked to speak, it is of little consequence to others in the class, who probably won't remember who spoke or what they said by the end of it. Whatever embarrassment is felt by the speaker has no long-term significance for anyone.

There are a number of things you can do to prepare yourself for the inevitable. First of all, it may help to organize and understand material like case analyses by stating out loud what it means and why (e.g. "The plaintiff X is suing the defendant Y for . . . because . . . [legal issue]. The issue in the case is . . . ; the holding is . . . ; and the rationale the court used to reach the holding is . . ."). It is generally useful to review reading assignments for ten or so minutes immediately prior to class. This will keep you sharp for discussion.

If you are asked to speak and have not read the relevant material or are unprepared to discuss it, you are better off saying so, rather than attempting to bluff. If, on the other hand, you have read the material but are unsure of what it means or how to answer the professor's question, it is best to explain why you are unsure rather than give the impression that you haven't completed the assignment.

Many students feel "unprepared" much of the time no matter how much studying they have done before class. Dealing with ambiguity is often much more significant than obtaining immediate clarity; the professor is probably more interested in the ambiguity than in the "correct" answer anyway.

If you are called on and are not quite sure of the question, you can ask that it be repeated or state what you believe the question entails before answering it. And keep in mind that when a student answers a question, even if the response is correct, the professor may not offer any positive feedback, or any feedback whatsoever. This is common when the Socratic method is being used, so don't feel that you have messed up just because you get no response from your teacher.

On the question of volunteering to speak in class, it is worth finding out what the professor's classroom and grading policies are, since some professors reward class participation and dock unprepared students. Sometimes consistent quality class participation will give a student a half-letter grade increase on his final grade, while consistent lack of preparation will lower a student's overall grade by half a letter value.

Finally, don't be afraid to ask questions in class. Rest assured that if you have a question about the material, at least a third of the class have a similar question but are just not asking it. Many professors proceed on the assumption that there is no such thing as a stupid question; if among such a bright group of people there is a question, it is possible that the material has not been communicated clearly or that the area is simply ambiguous. The degree to which ambiguity permeates the subject matter of law school cannot be overemphasized.

Tips for Classroom Success

The following tips are extracted from the material you have been reading and will help keep you on track in the law school classroom:

1. Be alert and ready to discuss the reading material; review it immediately before class so that it is fresh in your memory.

2. The goal of a class is generally to analyze, understand, and attempt to resolve issues or problems; correct "answers," if there are any, are of little consequence.

3. Learn to state and explain legal rules and principles with accuracy.

4. Don't lose sight of the "big picture" among the minutiae; ask yourself what the general significance of the case you are reading is and what does it add to your understanding of the rules and principles.

5. Accept the ambiguity in legal analysis and class discussion; classes are intended to be thought-provoking, perplexing, and difficult.

6. Review your notes from class later the same day. This will help you remember the material and will make preparing for finals easier. Additionally, a week's worth of notes should be reviewed at the end of the week.

7. No one class session will make or break you. Keep in mind how each class fits within the course overall.

8. Don't write down what other students say. Concentrate your notes on the professor's hypotheticals and emphasis in class, including cases and laws.

9. A simple but effective way of keeping yourself in touch with where the class is at any given time is to review the table of contents in the casebook.

10. If you don't use a laptop, don't sit next to someone who does. The constant tapping on the keys will drive you crazy and you may get a sense that they are writing down more than you. That is probably not true, but avoid the aggravation by sitting elsewhere.

11. If you attend class, you don't need to tape-record class. There are better uses of your time than to spend hours listening to the comments of students who were as confused as you were at the time you first dealt with the material in class.

Words and Language: Making Your Case

Words and language constitute some of the most significant aspects of law school learning. Those who successfully master legal terms and their use will find it easier to succeed in school and advance in the profession. One of the most important skills lawyers learn is how to argue a position or issue. Arguing, or advocacy, can take many different forms, but when you really think about it, there is only a limited number of possible arguments. Thus, whenever you are asked what the law, rule, or resolution of a problem is, you can always use one or a combination of the following arguments:

1. A prior case or statute (precedent) says so.

2. The proposed rule is not workable because a clear enough line cannot be drawn (the slippery slope).

3. The proposition is bad or wrong in itself; to do it is immoral.

4. The costs are greater than the benefits (efficiency).

5. The rule or approach should be adopted because it will deter bad behavior and lead to better results.

6. If you adopt the rule, the end of the Western world as we know it will occur; things will fall apart completely.

7. It is not our job; we don't do that kind of work (competency).

Here's how the above process might work as you prepare for a discussion in the area of criminal law:

"Should the death penalty serve as a form of punishment to a crime?"

A. Precedent

1. Pro-death penalty: The Supreme Court has consistently held that the death penalty is constitutional.

2. Anti-death penalty: The Supreme Court has held that the death penalty is unconstitutional in rape cases, and that mandatory death penalties are also unconstitutional.

B. The slippery slope argument

1. Anti-death penalty: Even if the death penalty is otherwise appropriate, the line cannot be drawn as

to who should get the death penalty and who should not. Some people plead out and do not get the death penalty, while their partners in crime end up being sentenced to death. In addition, statistics show that the death penalty is applied in a discriminatory manner.

   2. <u>Pro-death penalty:</u> The rules governing the death penalty, which provide for a consideration of both helpful and harmful factors by a fact-finder, are applied in a workable fashion.

C. The moral argument

   1. <u>Anti-death penalty:</u> It is wrong to kill (i.e., two wrongs don't make a right).

   2. <u>Pro-death penalty:</u> A person who kills another should himself be killed (i.e., an eye for an eye).

D. The efficiency argument

   1. <u>Anti-death penalty:</u> It is more cost-effective (that is, cheaper) to keep death–row inmates alive when you consider how much is spent on the appeals process.

   2. <u>Pro-death penalty:</u> Crowded jails lead to more severe housing problems.

E. Deterrence

   1. <u>Pro-death penalty:</u> The death penalty deters others from committing the crime of murder, and it certainly deters the defendant from ever killing again.

   2. <u>Anti-death penalty:</u> There is no good evidence that shows that the death penalty actually deters others from committing the crime of murder, and no evidence that any of those people who were put to death would have killed another person if kept alive for the rest of their lives in prison.

F. The gloom and doom argument

   1. <u>Pro-death penalty:</u> If there is no death penalty, people will start killing each other in greater numbers, and America will become a lawless society, reverting back to the wild, wild west.

2. <u>Anti-death penalty:</u> If the death penalty is widely used, America will become a barbaric society, where it is acceptable for the state to kill people, life is cheap, and no one respects our justice system anymore.

G. The competency argument

1. <u>Pro-death penalty:</u> It is up to the people, not the judges, to say whether or not there should be a death penalty, and the people want it.

2. <u>Anti-death penalty:</u> It is a constitutional question as to whether there should be a death penalty, and the popular opinion of the people is really irrelevant to what the Constitution says or means.

Professional Responsibility or Ethics

Almost every school requires that students take a class in legal ethics. Generally, this is in the second or third year, but some schools specifically include ethics in the first year. A legal ethics course deals not only with specific ethical issues, but also with general problems of professionalism. It may examine the attorney's responsibilities to the client, the court, and society at large. Students learn about a model statute, the American Bar Association's Model Rules of Professional Responsibility, and perhaps the code adopted by their respective states. They are also asked to negotiate various ethical dilemmas that they will face as lawyers.

CASE ANALYSIS

The primary tool used to teach legal reasoning in class is the appellate case report. This is an opinion by a judge or judges about a legal issue raised by one or more parties in an appeal. The opinions contained in casebooks are generally of the highest appellate courts of the states, or the federal courts of appeal and the United States Supreme Court, and are included for their legal significance or discussion of a particular issue or topic. Appellate case reports are important not only because they decide the issue for the parties in the case, but because they can be binding on how future lawsuits raising similar issues will be decided. This deference to prior decisions is the principle of precedental effect, also called state decisis. Sometimes only the majority opinion is reproduced in the casebook, but there may also be concurring opinions, in which the judge agrees with the conclusion but not the reasoning from which it has been derived, or dissenting opinions, in which the judge disagrees with the outcome of the case. There is usually more than one reasonable interpretation of any issue, hence the use of the word "opinion." Furthermore, if no reasonable basis for the dispute existed, it is likely that the case would not have been heard on appeal.

One focus of class discussion, then, is how to approach an issue analytically. And since judicial opinions are themselves subject to interpretation, their meanings will undoubtedly also provide focus for discussion. In addition, opinions present legal rules and principles, so you will probably also find yourself critiquing the court's application of these rules and principles. A case may also be compared to other cases or hypothetical situations. In this instance, you will apply the legal rule or principle of the case to different sets of facts in order to determine its meaning in different fact settings.

Both in and out of class, you should feel free to take positions contrary to the opinions you read. Students eventually learn that the holding of a case—the resolution of the issue—for the purpose of class discussion, is often of much less importance than the rationale or means by which the reviewing court evaluated the case in reaching its decision.

The Difference Between Interpreting a Case and a Statute

Decisions by judges interpret, and sometimes create, legal rules and principles. This body of decisional material is usually referred to as the common law. It is distinguished from another source of law in our society—the legislature. The legislature enacts statutes which are construed in and are the subject of many judicial opinions.

The method of interpreting a judicial decision is different from that of interpreting a statute. A judicial decision resolves a genuine case or controversy, and its holding should be limited to the facts presented. To the extent that the court addresses facts not present in the case, its pronouncements regarding those hypothetical facts are called dicta. Judges therefore do not extend their holdings to facts not presented in the actual case.

In refusing to reach questions not presented by the case, judges do not suggest that their holdings should be extended beyond those facts in the next case. On the contrary, judicial opinions are resources which are designed to be extended to subsequent cases. The quint-essential legal skill is to argue that the holdings of one case should or should not be extended to the facts of a new case. Whether a holding should be extended depends on the strength of the analogy between the decided case and the new case. The strength of the analogy is the subject of legal reasoning and legal arguments. Are the differences between the decided case and the new case relevant, or are the two cases sufficiently analogous that the holding of one should be extended to dispose of the other? Does the reasoning used by the judge in the decided case apply by analogy to the new case, or is that reasoning limited to the unique facts of the decided case? These questions form the essence of legal analysis.

In direct contrast, statutes cannot be interpreted by analogy. Statutes, generally speaking, are not designed to be extended beyond their terms. On the contrary, the overriding principle of statutory inter-pretation is that the inclusion of one term in a statute indicates the legislative intent to exclude other terms. Legislation is not the product of judicial reasoning; it is the product of compromise, a virtual contract struck between the legislative and competing constituencies. Faced with that carefully balanced political compromise, the courts have no power to extend a statute beyond its terms or to rewrite the statute in any way.

Addressing the Case:
Palsgraf v. Long Island R.R. Co.

Now let's return to your first class. We didn't mention it before, but it's torts. Remember, you and the other students are fidgeting nervously in your seats, and the professor is standing at the podium. You, yes you, are called upon to state the facts of *Palsgraf v. Long Island Rail Road Co.* The professor adds, "Why did the court rule against the plaintiff?" You skim the pertinent part of the case, which is before you, and clear your throat, ready to respond. Now, here's what a case looks like . . .

Palsgraf v. Long Island R.R. Co.
{248 N.Y. 339 (Ct. Appls. 1928)}

Cardozo, C.J. The plaintiff was standing on a platform of the defendant's railroad after having bought a ticket to go to Rockaway Beach. A train stopped at the station, bound for another place. Two men ran forward to catch it. One of the men reached the platform of the car without mishap, though the train was already moving. The other man, carrying a package, jumped aboard the car, but seemed unsteady, as if about to fall. A guard on the car, who had held the door open, reached forward to help him in, and another guard on the platform pushed him from behind. During this act, the package was dislodged, and fell onto the rails. The package was only about fifteen inches long, and was wrapped in newspaper. It contained fireworks, but there was nothing in its appearance to give notice of its contents. The fireworks exploded when they fell. The shock of the explosion threw down some scales at the other end of the platform many feet away. The scales struck the plaintiff, causing injuries for which she sued.

The conduct of the defendant's guard, if wrong in its relation to the holder of the package, was not a wrong in its relation to the plaintiff, standing far away. In relation to her it was not negligence at all.

[W]rong is defined in terms of the natural or probable, at least when unintentional . . . Here, by concession, there was nothing in the situation to suggest to the most cautious mind that the parcel wrapped in newspaper would spread wreckage through the station.

The judgment of the Appellate Division and that of the Trial Term should be reversed, and the complaint dismissed, with costs in all courts.

Exercise #9: Understanding
Palsgraf v. Long Island R.R. Co.

1. Who originally brought suit in this case?

2. What is the basis for this lawsuit?

3. Why did the court rule against Mrs. Palsgraf?

4. Does it matter how close to the scene of the explosion Mrs. Palsgraf was standing? Why?

5. A study of the facts of the case suggests that the fireworks made noise but did not cause the scales to become dislodged. If the scales were instead dislodged by a startled person standing on the platform, would that have made a difference to the outcome of the case? Why?

6. If the injured plaintiff had been walking outside the station and was not a passenger, would the railroad now owe her a duty of care?

Answers

1. The plaintiff who brought suit initially was Mrs. Palsgraf.

2. The lawsuit was filed in order to recover damages for injuries suffered when the scales fell on the plaintiff.

3. The court held that the defendant railroad did not owe Mrs. Palsgraf a duty of care and, while the defendant's conduct may have been wrong, it was not wrong in relation to the plaintiff.

4. The fact that the plaintiff stood on the platform well away from the explosion was significant—it indicated that she was outside the zone in which the explosion could reasonably be expected to affect her adversely.

5. If a startled person had dislodged the scales as a result of the explosion, there is no additional reason to believe a duty of care would be created.

6. If the plaintiff had been walking outside the station, there is even less of a chance that a duty would be created, since the defendant has less of a reason to foresee the need to protect passersby.

Reading and Briefing Cases

A major task for law students in preparing for class is reading and briefing cases. This involves writing a synopsis of each case by extracting its important components. The word "brief" should be taken literally; the work of first-year law students often turns out to be excessively long. The cases to be briefed are usually appeals. An appellate opinion is a written report describing the resolution of a legal issue and the reasoning behind the decision.

As we said earlier, the cases in the law school casebook often do not contain the entire opinion, but only selected text. In addition, parts of the same case may be used for entirely different substantive courses. Thus, a case in a torts text may also appear in a constitutional law book on an entirely different question.

There are many ways to organize a case brief, but certain information is generally included. Important aspects of a case include the legal issue (the question the court must decide), the applicable facts, and the procedural background (which courts have heard the case, their holdings, and the rationale for each of their decisions.

One way to create a super-condensed version of a case is to ask the questions: "Who is suing whom? For what? On what basis?" Furthermore, it is helpful to assign a case a descriptive word or phrase. For example, *Roe v. Wade* is "the trimester-abortion-approach case," and the case of *New York Times v. Sullivan* is "the actual-malice-standard libel case." Without such descriptive labels, it is often difficult to distinguish one case from another. These brief descriptions will also help you recall the material more efficiently on the final examination.

The Major Components of a Case Brief

Most case briefs follow the following format:

1. Case name
2. Court deciding the case
3. Date of decision
4. Parties to the case
5. Nature of the case (tort, criminal, corporate, etc.)
6. Procedure (how the case came to this appellate court)
7. Important facts
8. The issue (the question presented on appeal)
9. The holding (answers the issue)
10. The court's rationale in reaching its holding
11. Dicta (the rules and principles not essential to the holding)
12. Precedental significance of the case
13. Concurrence
14. Dissent

The Issue

The issue in a case presents the conflict which must be resolved by the court. It can be described broadly or narrowly, depending on how many of the facts are included. A broad issue offers a general statement about the abstract legal question raised on appeal and is framed in the form of a question. For example, "Whether a promise is still binding without legal consideration?" A narrow issue applies the law to the specific facts of a case. The more facts included in the issue, the narrower it will be. An illustration of a narrow legal issue is: "Whether a promise to give a gift for a person's twenty-fifth birthday in the form of a bright red BMW convertible is binding on the promisor when the promisee was not required to do or cease to do anything in return?"

Exercise #10: Identifying the issue

Read through the following excerpt from *Wood v. Lucy, Lady Duff-Gordon* 222 N.Y. 88, 118 N.E. 214 (Ct. Appls. 1917).

Cardozo, J. The defendant styles herself "a creator of fashions." Her favor helps a sale. Manufacturers of dresses, millinery, and like articles are glad to pay for a certificate of her approval. The things she designs, fabrics, parasols, and whatnot, have a new value in the public mind when issued in her name. She employed the plaintiff to help her turn this vogue into money. He was to have the exclusive right, subject always to her approval, to place her endorsement on the designs of others. He was also to have the exclusive right to place her own designs on sale, or to license others to market them. In return she was to have one-half of "all profits and revenues" derived from any contracts he might make. The exclusive right was sold for at least one year from April 1, 1915, and thereafter from year to year unless terminated by notice of ninety days. The plaintiff says that he kept the contract on his part and that the defendant broke it. She placed her endorsement on fabrics, dresses, and millinery without his knowledge, and withheld the profits. He sues her for the damages, and the case comes here on demurrer [after the complaint was dismissed because the court found the contract was not binding on the plaintiff].

Identify the legal issue from the above excerpt.

_____

_____

_____

Answer

A broad issue for this case would read something like: Whether a contract providing one party with the exclusive right to sell the fashion apparel of the other party is enforceable?

The Facts

In a case brief, only the facts contained in the case which are important to the resolution of the issue on appeal should be included. In a murder prosecution, for example, the murder weapon may or may not be relevant to the appeal. If it is not, its existence can be omitted from the brief.

The Procedure

The procedure describes how the case reached the appellate court in question. Sometimes the case would have been to trial, then to one or more of the lower appellate courts, before it reached its current posture. The procedure is something like a road map of the case.

The Holding

The holding of the case essentially answers the issue presented on appeal. Sometimes, judges state the holding expressly, saying something like, " The holding in this matter is . . . ." Often, however, students must infer what the holding is by the way the court has resolved the question. For example, the holding may be expressed as follows: "For the reasons stated, we cannot agree with the appellate court that the appropriate standard of care was met in this case. Only a physician with a sufficient expertise in the area can testify, not any physician who has successfully completed medical school. Reversed and remanded."

The Rationale

The rationale is the reasoning by which the court reached its conclusion; it is often the most important part of a case. Judges reason using two primary methods—precedent and policy. Precedent may involve prior case decisions, known as the common law, or statutes. Judges also use policy arguments such as morality, administrability (that is, feasibility), efficiency (cost-benefit analysis), or competency (asking whose job it is to decide the matter).

Dicta

Some judges offer an opinion about matters beyond the scope of the issue presented in the case. These opinions are called dicta. Dicta are of lesser significance and are non-binding in later cases. However, they can be instructive and they may provide guidance in later cases.

Concurring Opinions
A concurrence is written by a judge who agrees with the majority opinion about how a case should be decided, but who differs in her rationale. The concurrence explains this difference.

Dissenting Opinions
A judge writes a dissenting opinion to disagree with the majority decision in a case. In this opinion, the judge explains why he decided that the majority decision was incorrect.

Case-briefing Tips

1. Locate the issue and the holding first, in order to determine what the case is about.

2. Ask what the overall significance of the case is. Why is the professor assigning it? This keeps the big picture in mind.

3. State out loud briefly what the case is about. What are the issues and holdings? If you cannot repeat these statements out loud, it's as if you have no knowledge of it.

4. Don't just rewrite a case in your brief; summarize and condense it in a useable fashion. It should be like the drive-through in fast-food restaurants—"to go."

"I am so happy here. Unlike some of my friends at other law schools, I enjoyed my first year. People here are truly supportive——they are here to learn and work hard when they need to, but the atmosphere is relaxed and friendly. My only regret is that law school is only three years. Maybe I'll get an LLM."

—2L, University of Virginia

Types of Cases: State or Federal Court?

A case may have been initiated in the state court system, which has one or more levels of trial courts. If there is more than one level, the difference between them is based on the significance of the issues being contested or the amount of money at issue. Many states have several levels of appellate courts, culminating in the highest state court. The highest court is often called the State Supreme Court, but the names may vary from state to state. New York, for example, calls its trial courts the Supreme Court, and its highest appeals court the New York Court of Appeals.

The federal court system essentially has three levels. The Federal District Court is the trial court and handles the equivalent of some appeals such as claims for *habeas corpus* by prisoners. The appellate court is the Circuit Court of Appeals, of which there are eleven plus the District of Columbia. Federal Circuits and the United States Supreme Court are also federal courts.

THE STATE AND FEDERAL COURT SYSTEMS

There are essentially fifty-two individual court systems in the United States. Each state has its own court system, the District of Columbia has a system, and there is a federal judicial system. The state courts handle the majority of the nation's caseload. Jurisdiction refers to a court's power to decide cases based on its authority over the parties and the subject matter of the case. State courts are courts of general jurisdiction, which basically gives them the authority to hear any kind of case. The federal courts have limited jurisdiction, meaning that they may hear only disputes which qualify as "cases or controversies" as stated in Article III of the Constitution. Federal jurisdiction falls into two categories, those cases pertaining to federal subject matter, and those cases involving parties warranting federal attention. The federal courts hear cases falling within the judicial authority of the United States as provided by the Constitution and Congress. Federal courts mainly try cases which involve federal law, the Constitution, or treaties, and cases which involve states, the United States, or citizens of different states.

The Federal Courts

The United States Supreme Court

The United States Supreme Court is the highest, most powerful judicial body in the land. It consists of nine justices who are nominated to the Court by the president and confirmed by the Senate for life. Article III of the United States Constitution provides the Court with its original and appellate jurisdiction. Original jurisdiction is the Court's power to hear and decide a case from the beginning. The Supreme Court only has original jurisdiction over two types of cases: those in which a state is a party, and those cases involving a representative of a foreign nation. Congress may not broaden or narrow the Supreme Court's original jurisdiction, but the Court's appellate jurisdiction is subject to changes by Congress.

The Supreme Court maintains broad power over the federal judicial system. It supervises the lower courts and reviews lower court decisions. The Supreme Court grants parties the opportunity to present their case through certiorari, meaning discretionary appeal, and by direct appeal. The Supreme Court receives many petitions for certiorari each year, but hears only a small percentage of these. Additionally, the Supreme Court acts as the final voice over state court case issues dealing with federal law. The Court also has the power to propose rules of procedure for the federal court system.

Federal Circuit Courts of Appeal

There are thirteen United States Courts of Appeal. These courts constitute the middle of the three-tiered federal judicial system. Losing parties in federal courts of appeal may petition the Supreme Court to review the appellate decision by certiorari, or direct appeal as of right.

Federal District Court

The federal district courts constitute the lowest tier of the three-tiered federal judicial system. The system consists of ninety-four districts. There is at least one district in every state and no district crosses state lines. The district courts hear both criminal and civil cases. Losing parties in federal district court cases may appeal to the appeals court in the circuit or geographic area in which the federal district court is located.

The State Courts

State Supreme Court

As mentioned earlier, the states call their highest courts by different names. For our purposes, we will refer to the court of last resort in each individual state as the State Supreme Court. This court makes the final decisions on cases it chooses to hear. Those cases it denies are subject to the decision of the state court of appeals.

State Court of Appeals

State courts of appeal are intermediate-level courts which review the proceedings of the state trial courts in order to determine whether those courts have committed any error in applying the law to the facts of the case. Any party who loses at trial has the right to have the judgment reviewed by the appellate court.

State Circuit (Trial) Court

These courts are distributed geographically throughout each state. Cases tried here may involve civil claims or criminal prosecution. These courts deal with issues of fact and criminal and civil liability.

Exercise #11: Reading a state case

Read through *People v. Bowen and Rouse* (10 Mich. App. 1, 158 N.W. 2d 794 [Ct. Appls 1968]) and answer the questions which follow.

Levin, Judge. Defendants, Sherrel Bowen and William Rouse, appeal their convictions of attempted larceny in a building.

On January 19, 1965, at approximately 8 p.m., the defendants and two female companions were admitted to the home of one Matilda Gatzmeyer, an 80-year-old woman. The defendants' car was observed parked in front of Miss Gatzmeyer's residence and a neighbor, believing the defendants to have designs upon her property, called the police. Two police officers arrived and entered the home along with the neighbor. The defendants were found in the rear of the house near or on the basement steps. The two female companions were seated on either side of Miss Gatzmeyer, apparently engaged with her in conversation.

Defendant Rouse seated himself within a foot of the television, and some time thereafter one of the police officers spotted under the television set two rings belonging to Miss Gatzmeyer. The neighbor testified she found a necklace on the staircase near where defendant Bowen had been standing.

There was sufficient evidence to support the defendants' conviction of attempt to commit larceny.

[However,] we do find error in the judge's failure to charge the jury properly on the necessity of finding an overt act [in furtherance of the larceny]. Not only did the trial judge fail to charge the jury at all concerning the necessity of finding an overt act, but he also incorrectly charged that the jury could convict if it found that the defendants came to or entered Miss Gatzmeyer's house with the intention of committing larceny.

Reversed and remanded for a new trial.

1. Why is this a state case?
2. What would make it a federal case?
3. What are the important facts? Why?
4. What is the issue in the case?
5. How did the court decide the issue?

Answers

1. The action was brought in state court because the defendants allegedly violated the state's criminal laws.

2. It would become a federal case if it occurred on federal land or otherwise was a violation of federal law.

3. The fact that the jewelry was found near the defendants in places not left by its owner indicates that, without apparent permission to do so, the defendants took and carried away, until the police came, property of another, Miss Gatzmeyer, without any evidence of an intent to return it.

4. Did the trial judge err in not instructing the jury that in order to convict, the jury must find that an "overt" act occurred (meaning an act sufficiently close to the commission of the completed crime that it is symbolic of the crime)?

5. The court held that the trial judge did not accurately instruct the jury on "the necessity of finding an overt act ... "

Exercise #12: Reading a federal case

Read through *Kotteakos v. United States* (328 U.S. 750 [1946]) and answer the questions which follow.

The defendant was tried along with thirty-one other people on the charge of participating in a single conspiracy to obtain loans by false and fraudulent applications to the Federal Housing Administration. The defendant was convicted and he appealed. The Circuit Court of Appeals found that there was no single thirty-two-person conspiracy, and that it was error to convict the defendant of conspiring with thirty-one other people. The appeals court also found, however, that the error was harmless, and affirmed the conviction. The Supreme Court reversed, stating: "One difficulty with [the view that the single conspiracy theory was harmless] is that the trial court itself was confused in the charge which it gave to guide the jury in deliberation."

1. What makes this a federal case?

2. Why does the heading list Kotteakos first?

3. How did the case get to the Supreme Court? (That is, what happened in the courts below?)

4. What are the important facts of the case?

5. What issue did the Supreme Court face in the case?

6. How did the Court resolve the issue?

Answers

1. While states enact the majority of the criminal laws, federal statutes proscribe certain conduct as criminal. Here, the defendants allegedly violated federal housing law.

2. Kotteakos lost in the previous court, the Circuit Court of Appeals.

3. The defendant was convicted upon trial in the Federal District Court and appealed. While the appellate court found that it was an error to convict the defendant of conspiring with thirty-one other people in a single conspiracy, the court also found that this error was not so significant that a new trial or the equivalent should

be ordered. The court subsequently affirmed the conviction and the defendant appealed to the United States Supreme Court.

4. The important facts are: Defendant tried with thirty-one people on single conspiracy charge to falsely obtain loans. Defendant convicted. On appeal, court found harmless error in finding a single 32-person conspiracy—affirmed. Supreme Court reversed. Found jury charge to be confusing.

5. The issue before the Supreme Court was: Whether it was harmless error to find that a 32-person conspiracy existed.

6. The Supreme Court agreed with the appeals court that the trial judge erred, but disagreed that the error was harmless to the defendant. Consequently, it reversed the conviction.

OUTSIDE THE CLASSROOM

Time Management

Managing one's time well is a top priority in law school, where it seems that reading and understanding even one case can take forever. The pressures are great, but with sensible planning, everyone can get through law school and still have time to enjoy themselves. One's weekly schedule needs to balance class, study, sleep, and self-maintenance. Here is an example of a weekly plan:

Monday/Wednesday/Friday

Torts (9:00 a.m.-10:00 a.m.); Contracts (10:30 a.m.-11:30 a.m.)

Civil procedure (1:00 p.m.-2:00 p.m.)

Legal/Research (2:15 p.m.-3:15 p.m.) (Fridays only)

Study (8:00 a.m.-9:00 a.m.)

Lunch (noon-1:00 p.m.)

Gym (2:30 p.m.-4:00 p.m.)

Study (6:00 p.m.-11:00 pm)

Tuesday/Thursday

> Criminal law (9:00 a.m.-10:15 a.m.)
>
> Property (10:30 p.m.-11:45 p.m.)
>
> Study (1:00 p.m.-5:00 p.m.)
>
> Dinner (5:00 p.m.-6:30 p.m.)
>
> Study (6:00 p.m.-11:00 p.m.)

Weekends should be a combination of study and personal time. Keep up with your work, but don't compromise the need to stay healthy—physically and psychologically.

"Beer and softball might send the message students are academically slack: untrue. Some of the softball diamond's superstars write on the Law Review. Students here have realized that a balanced lifestyle gives you more energy."

—1L, University of Virginia

Some useful books on time management:

1. *Planning Work & Time*, Merrill Douglas

2. *A New Strategy for Time Management*, Phil Van Aukin

3. *Time Management: Clearing the Stacks*, Ginger Trumfio

4. *Are You Managing Your Time or is Time Managing You?* Scott Romeo

Study Guides

There is a huge array of study guides and various other learning aids available to assist law students in their studies. Most of these are commercially prepared and are sold in law school bookstores. As a rule of thumb, study guides should be used to supplement your regular texts; they are *not* substitutes. In the first year, you will learn to read and digest cases and to spot and analyze issues. A study guide will help you understand the rules, but will not teach you how to best spot an issue, or analyze that issue.

Study guides range from videotapes and audiotapes to folders of information and books. Perhaps the best way to determine which resource is best for you is to browse through the materials on reserve in your school's library. You should bear in mind what your professor wants in each class and whether or not the professor's emphasis is consistent with that of the study guides. Some professors recommend study guides or outside resource materials, others ignore the subject altogether.

If a professor recommends a study guide, it will probably be the most complete resource available, often called a "hornbook." Such books tend to be written in a scholarly fashion, contain more information and be more nuanced than most other materials. On the other hand, they are often also more difficult to read.

There are many materials available which condense the rules and principles into unambiguous and palatable forms. These popular books are good for finding things out quickly, but they tend to oversimplify the subject matter and mislead you in the process. It is always necessary to read the assigned material thoroughly before using a study guide. Preparing with a study guide first may cause you to miss points which are addressed in the casebook and later in class discussion.

Note that the authors of study guides often disagree with each other on the statement of particular rules and principles and may also differ from your professor about how to phrase, state, or explain a particular doctrine. When this occurs, remember who will be the judge on the final exam—your own professor. Your professor's interpretation of the rules governs. In fact, you'd be well advised to remember that you take the professor, *not* the course. All teachers will emphasize certain topics and not cover others. Study guides cover it all and that's to your benefit. But never confuse an outside resource with a professor's own emphasis.

So, how do you use study guides? Here are some tips to help you get the best out of them:

- Read the guide's analysis of cases and subjects, and do some of the problems. In this way you will know whether you understand the legal rules and principles.

- The best way to answer the problems in a study guide is to simulate the final exam, writing out your responses as you would in the actual exam.

- You will know your study guide was helpful if you can state and explain the rules and principles out loud. Reading about the rules and principles is not the same as understanding them.

- In addition to reviewing the problem in a study guide, make up your own. If you can make up examples about legal rules and principles, you will be better able to understand and spot the issues dealing with those rules on exams.

Some of the more popular study guides include:

1. Emmanuel's *On the Law*. A detailed outline of the law. A book prepared for each course.

2. Gilbert's *On the Law*. An alternative outline. Less chatty than Emmanuel's.

3. *Sum and Substance*. Another outline of the course.

4. West's *Hornbook* series. Large, detailed narratives of each area of the law.

5. West's *Black Letter Law* series. A detailed outline of the law.

6. *The Law In a Flash*. Cards reminiscent of how you learned mathematics adapted for law school.

7. *In a Nutshell* series. Small paperbacks providing detailed narratives of the law.

8. *Case Note* legal briefs. If you have no time to brief, here is someone's else's version. Case note texts are casebook specific. Warning: the case note author doesn't always agree with your professor's recitation of the facts or issue and some briefs have been known to be just plain wrong! But in a jam they can come in handy. Best suggestion: be prepared and brief it yourself!

9. Black's *Law Dictionary*. Lawyers have their own language. It helps to be able to look things up. This is the classic text.

10. Gilbert's *Legal Dictionary*. Gilbert's produces a smaller, easily transportable resource you can take to class.

11. *Legalines*. Another form of class outline. More to the point and less chatty than Emmanuel or West's *Black Letter* series.

12. Emanuel's *Flashcards*. Just like *Law in a Flash*. A popular item.

You are well advised to wait until you've been attending classes for a few weeks before deciding which resources to buy. As a first-year student you will have many second- and third-year students offering you their used books. Resist the temptation! You just won't have a handle on your personal preference until you've been in class for a while. Experience the course, the professor, and the material, and get a sense of what will work best for *you*.

Student Outlines

In addition to commercially available outlines and materials, many students prepare their own course outlines. These include the essential elements of the cases, what the professor has said about those cases, and how they apply in different situations.

Writing your own course outlines has several advantages. Besides being a way of "imprinting" the rules on your mind, it is another way to understand and organize the material. Because organization is so important, outlines can be extremely useful, especially as finals approach.

The following is a brief excerpt from a law student's torts outline. Consider whether this format might work for you:

I. Negligent Infliction of Emotional Distress—traditionally, P must suffer physical harm to recover

A. <u>Dillon</u>-(min.) allowed recovery to one not physically harmed and outside of zone of danger; has been rejected by majority of states in favor of zone of danger approach, and questioned in its own state (CA)

B. extra-sensitive P—eggshell P rule applies unless D does not owe P a duty of care

C. nervous shock in cumulative trauma cases—some courts require that physical harm must be suffered by P, plus the emotional harm must be foreseeable (D knew or should have known his actions would cause P severe emotional shock/harm); others don't require physical harm anymore (<u>Molimen</u>)

D. claims for nervous shock following the inaccurate transmission of information have been allowed

II. Defamation: Prima Facie Case

   A. defamatory statement (tending to lower P's reputation) about this P—as long as persons to whom it is published could reasonably interpret it in a sense defamatory

     1. <u>of & concerning the P</u>-when P not mentioned by name she bears the burden of proving that it refers to her (it's a jury question) [D argues that no reasonable person would associate the character w/the P]

     2. <u>group libel</u>-cannot defame a group. Exception: where there is clearly identifiable one person in the group who fits the description

     3. <u>ambiguity</u>
       i. doctrine of mitior sensus-if ambiguous, construe it in least derogatory manner

     4. maj.-natural & obvious meaning

     5. min.-when words have two meanings, construe in more lenient sense

     6. inducement & innuendo-P must prove extrinsic facts, not included in publication, which, if taken together w/publication, produce an innuendo

     7. <u>statements of opinion</u>-alone do not suffice. But when they appear to be based on knowledge of facts and an express allegation of those facts would be defamatory, then it's actionable (e.g., "I think X is a blackmailer")

B. publication-communication to 3rd person, intention-
    ally or negligently (3rd person must understand it);
    3rd person need not believe defamatory matter

Study Groups

Study groups assist students by providing a "live" forum in which
to discuss course-related issues, but they also provide support and
encouragement, which may otherwise be minimal in the law school
environment. When functioning properly, study groups can be extremely helpful to participants. How well a study group works depends
of course on the personalities of the people who make it up. If you
are thinking about forming or joining a study group, consider whether
the other students are like you. Do they, for example, have the same
level of anxiety, intensity, and approach to law school? Questions
like this often become very significant as the semester wears on,
exams approach, and patience grows thin.

You should always wait at least a couple of months into your
studies before joining a study group, the reasons being:

1. You need time to meet and find other students who
   will complement your own style and approach to your
   work. If you jump in too soon, you may find yourself
   with people whose work and study habits are quite
   different from your own, which will probably make
   working together difficult.

2. You need to have spent some time studying and learning
   the material before you are ready to integrate it into
   discussion.

3. You may prefer to work alone, but won't recognize
   this at first.

So, how many people should you have in a study group? Somewhere
between two and five probably works best. Mold your group carefully
so that it is made up of people who will work well together, support
each other, and promote each other's success.

> *"I am amazed because, before I entered law school, I thought it would be the ultimate in competition. I was wrong, because Brooklyn Law students are like one big family, willing to help and support one another."*
> —**1L, Brooklyn Law**

Tutoring and Academic Assistance Programs

In some law schools tutoring by higher level students is offered to first-year students. The quality of this kind of help can vary widely. A good tutor, however, will provide valuable help and support to the new student: what is important in the first courses; what are the good study guides; tips on drafting outlines and taking finals. The connections first-year students make with upper classmen may also lead to advice on job hunting, honors programs, and other law school activities. Other schools offer attorney-mentors to first-year students. These mentors generally provide suggestions and advice on broader issues such as those addressed in this book.

Bar Review Course

You have only been in law school a couple of weeks when you notice a table set up in the student lounge—it is staffed by people talking about bar review courses. They spout off about how much you can save by registering with a company early. They tell you all the benefits of their program, none of which means anything to you, since you've not yet taken even one round of finals. To make matters worse, one of your classmates enrolls in the company's class (which won't begin for three years) and starts hassling you to join the same program. (If you register early you can become one of their on-campus salespeople and either save money or receive cash back for convincing others to enroll.)

Well, don't feel pressured. No matter how many people badger you to sign up, you don't have to decide anything until much later in the game. Yes, it is true that you will save some money by deciding early, but what is a couple of hundred dollars after all the money you will have spent by the end of your studies anyway? And who needs the stress of deciding which bar review course to take while still worrying about first-year finals?

THE BOOK STOPS HERE: THE AGE OF COMPUTER RESEARCH

The days of research by book are (thank goodness) mostly over. The computer age has hit the legal field, and lawyers can now conduct their legal case research through computer networks.

LEXIS/NEXIS

LEXIS/NEXIS is the oldest full-text computer research service for the legal and business fields. It consists of the full text of all reported cases dating back fifty years, and many cases which occured prior to that time, the full text of state and federal statutes and constitutions, various state and federal administrative and regulatory materials, and many secondary legal authorities such as law reviews and restatements. NEXIS, the LEXIS companion, offers an array of full-text news and business publications. Every database is full-text searchable, which means you can search for any word or phrase and find every document containing that word or phrase. Information on LEXIS/NEXIS is organized by "libraries" which contain "files."

LEXIS/NEXIS offers software to students at no cost so they can perform computer-assisted legal research at home. Law schools also have LEXIS/NEXIS capabilities set up in their computer labs. Students are assigned a password with which to log in; however, this lapses each summer unless you notify LEXIS/NEXIS services. When you graduate, your password will no longer be valid. For a practicing attorney the service is no longer free.

These computer-assisted legal research services are quick and user friendly, making legal research a breeze. It is still necessary, however, to learn how to do manual research properly, since not every law firm has the financial resources available to support a staff using LEXIS or another commonly used service, Westlaw. While it will be back to the books for most of you, certainly you will learn computer research skills during one of your writing classes.

WESTLAW

Westlaw is the legal computer research service provided by the West Publishing Company. This service provides access to a wide variety of information such as cases, statutes, codes, rules, administrative decisions, articles, periodicals, and other secondary material. The information is divided into various databases for quick and easy access. Searching for material is done by typing in key words and phrases which most accurately describe the information you are looking for. The goal is to narrow a search efficiently so that you only receive applicable material. Westlaw offers software to students, free of charge, for home use. Additionally, schools maintain Westlaw capabilities in their computer labs. Students are assigned a personal password for research purposes and must notify Westlaw services when they plan to use it over the summer. Your student password expires on graduation from law school, when the service is no longer free.

CHAPTER 4

The Exam Game: Playing to Win

INTRODUCTION

A law school exam is unlike any exam you have seen before. Moreover, your grades in law school will probably depend entirely on one final examination in each course. Generally, there are no midterms, no graded written assignments, and there is no credit for class participation. So, your success in law school will usually depend on how well you perform on that one final course exam. The good news is that there is a methodology for taking law school exams—a formula for success, if you will. If followed, the techniques outlined in this chapter will help you perform better on exams. In addition to the overall methodolgy you will learn, we have included specific tips and strategies that you will need to remember. In the heat of battle, it is easy to forget such small tips and strategies, so review and practice them until they become second nature.

Law school exams are typically largely or entirely composed of essays which present lengthy and convoluted hypothetical fact patterns raising a wide variety of legal issues. "Issue spotters," as they are called, ask students to analyze the facts, spot the issues raised by those facts, and apply the law and legal theories to those facts in order to reach some likely legal outcome. While issue spotters are the mainstay of law school exams, they may also include multiple-choice questions, short answers, and broader policy questions. Such questions often supplement the issue spotter. But even multiple-choice questions in law school are unlike the kind you saw in college. In law school, you should not be surprised to see a multiple-choice question with either ten different choices to select from, or with two or three correct answers, that is, correct in one way or another. Law professors are notorious for listing answers which begin: "True, but only if . . . " or "False, unless . . . " Sound like a nightmare? You're right. You need to know the law inside out so that when you are faced with a multiple-choice exam, you can recognize every nuance, exception, and possibility that may come into play.

"The first semester was hell! As a 1L, you are given little direction and have virtually no sense of how you are doing. It all comes down to that one exam. Pretty scary."
—2L, John Marshall

THE METHODOLOGY

Time Management and Organization

Time pressure obviously plays a significant role during examinations. While a three- or four-hour exam (the length of first-year exams is loosely based on the number of credit hours of a course) may appear to provide ample time to answer the questions, never be fooled. Your judgment regarding how to allocate your time is crucial, and the best way to get a handle on this is by taking a series of practice exams under simulated conditions.

Here are a few time-management and organizational pointers for taking exams in law school:

- When you receive the exam, take a few deep breaths—feel your lungs fill, hold the breath for a few seconds, and slowly exhale. This will help you relax.

- Skim through the exam questions.

- Note the number of questions and the point value assigned to each one. If there are no point values assigned, each question is of equal value.

- Now allocate your time. There are two types of time allocation you should consider. First, there is the "per question" time allocation, which requires you to determine the amount of time you will spend on each question. For example, if a question represents 40 percent of the total points of the exam, then you should allocate 40 percent of the total time to answering that question. Be careful not to get so caught up on one question that you have to race through the remaining questions.

The second type of time allocation you should consider is the internal "issue" time allocation. This is the time you allocate to the issues within a given question. The larger or more debatable issues will generally take more time than smaller, less complex issues. For example, in torts, a general negligence issue will require more time than a specific issue like battery. The latter is concrete and easy to tackle; the former is a broad concept consisting of several components.

- If you have the flexibility to answer questions out of order, move to those you feel you can answer with the least amount of stress. Otherwise, begin at the first question.

- The first fifteen to twenty minutes should be dedicated to organizing and preparing your answer. Don't even think about writing until you have spent at least 25 percent of your allocated time organizing and preparing. Here's how it works:

  — Read the question and identify what we refer to as the "call of the question." That is, the question you are being asked to answer. This is usually found at the end of the hypothetical fact pattern which constitutes the exam question. Identifying the call of a question enables you to place the fact pattern in perspective and provides you with a framework for reading the question.

  — Skim the question to get a basic feel and understanding of the *facts*. Do not mark up your paper or try to spot issues.

  — Go back and reread the fact pattern slowly and carefully. Now is the time to *issue spot*. Issue spotting is the process of identifying the legal issues that are raised or triggered by certain facts. For example, in torts, if someone in the fact pattern grabs someone else's arm, this fact triggers the issue of battery. And note that to spot legal issues you must have a masterful command of the rules of law. As you spot issues (that is, facts that give rise to an issue), underline those facts and identify the issue by making a notation in the margin. Use abbreviations whenever possible in order to save time.

— Then reread the call of the question. It is still not time to begin writing your answer even though by now you may have a near uncontrollable urge to do so. In fact, don't be surprised to see others around you writing frantically. But resist the temptation yourself!

— Now, using scratch paper or the inside cover of your blue book, draft a brief but detailed outline of the answer you intend to write. This is where your outlining skills will come in handy. You may want to consider using the IRAC method (see below) to outline your answer.

— Then you may calmly, legibly, and efficiently draft your answer.

The "IRAC" Method

To organize the analysis for an exam response, many students use what is called the "IRAC" method. IRAC is a mnemonic device that stands for "Issue—Rule—Analysis—Conclusion." Unfortunately, while students regularly use the pertinent words, they rarely apply the method correctly or completely.

The "IRAC" method divides the answer into parts, thereby creating a framework for analysis and encouraging a step-by-step approach. By employing IRAC, you will pay greater attention to important details. And in the law, the details which distinguish one particular fact scenario from others is the very basis upon which lawyers argue their cases. This method of analysis is not unlike what you will do as a lawyer.

The Issue

The issue captures and presents the legal question raised by the fact scenario described in the exam question. In your answer, you will usually phrase the issue by beginning "Whether . . . . " So, for example, some "issues" might include: whether Bob's conduct constituted battery; whether the trial court properly instructed the jury about Bob's alleged burglary; whether Sally's conduct, even if true, constituted the intentional infliction of emotional distress.

Rule

This component identifies and defines what rule (or rules) of law are applicable to the fact scenario and the legal issue raised. For example, in torts, negligence requires: duty of care; a breach of that duty; causation; and injuries to a plaintiff. The facts of the particular case are not discussed at this point, but are considered in the analysis.

Analysis (Application of the law to the facts)

Analysis means applying the law to the specific facts in the issue spotter. Analysis therefore requires knowing both the general legal rules and principles and the specific facts of a case or hypothetical. This component examines whether and how the legal rules are met by the facts of the particular case. It is here that the three most important words on a law school exam, and perhaps in law school, come into play: "In this case . . . ." The heart of your grade is *not* centered on the outcome, it is focused on the analysis. Remember, you can get an "A" regardless of the position you take on how the case should resolve.

Conclusion

This part of the answer is usually the least important. The conclusion simply indicates the likely resolution of the issue or, put another way, the outcome of the analysis as you see it. For example, it may simply be: "Therefore, since the state law discriminates based on national origin and fails to satisfy strict scrutiny, the law would most likely be unconstitutional."

Several of my professors gave us an open-book exam. That meant we could use our textbooks, study aids, and anything else we wanted, so long as it was not a human being. Guess what? Nothing helped! Exams aren't just about memorizing material. It's analyze, analyze, analyze."

—2L, Loyola, LA

WHAT COUNTS ON EXAMS

Okay, you have the method down. But before you try it out, read through the following additional information.

Read Carefully

Taking exams requires careful reading. All too often, students miss issues or misread questions, particularly the "call of the question." Misreading leads to incorrect analyses and, more importantly, a reduction in points.

Spot Issues, not just Concrete Violations

Students frequently approach issues thinking in terms of right and wrong; that is, they focus on discovering issues that give rise to concrete "correct" answers. Keep in mind that the issue spotter is there to measure your ability to evaluate and analyze legal questions, not to see if you can find a correct answer. Ambiguity is often an intentional part of an examination and issues are hidden within that ambiguity. Credit is given for addressing legal issues that are reasonably raised by the fact pattern. Even if it ultimately appears that no legal obligations are created or breached, that is, there is no crime, tort, or contract, you should still address and write about the issue. It is a skill to determine which issues you should include and which you should leave out. One rule of thumb is, when in doubt, mention it, if only in passing (for example, "The defendant also may be charged with burglary, although it is not likely because . . . ").

SAMPLE EXAMINATION QUESTIONS

Question I (40 minutes)

Teenagers Mary and Monique were bored after a long day at the beach. On their way home, they decided to break into a big, mysterious house on the corner to steal the magnificent art collection it contained. On the way to the house, Mary stole a flashlight from a local convenience store because the sun had set. Once at the house, Mary stayed in the car to stand guard. Suddenly, she remembered that she had to meet her brother to help him stash some cash from a robbery, so she left. Meanwhile, Monique broke into the house and, to her surprise, there was no art collection. In fact, it looked like a warehouse. It contained thousands of computer parts. Monique hated computers, and began to leave. All of a sudden, she heard a noise—behind her was a killer dog. She took out her unregistered handgun and shot at the dog in self-defense. Her hollow-point bullets killed the dog and, unbeknownst to Monique, also its owner, Fred, who was hiding just beyond it.

What crimes, if any, have Mary and Monique likely committed? Discuss.

Answer

Mary and Monique may be guilty of several crimes, including conspiracy to commit larceny of art work, larceny of a flashlight, attempted burglary, felony murder, and depraved heart murder.

1. Whether Mary and Monique committed conspiracy to commit larceny (Issue)

Both Mary and Monique may be found guilty of conspiracy to commit the crime of larceny of the house (Conclusion). Conspiracy at common law requires the act of an agreement to commit a crime and the mental state of an intent to commit the crime and the intent to agree (Rule).

If this is the case, Mary and Monique agreed to steal the art work, that is, to commit the crime of larceny, because the facts stated that they decided to steal the "magnificent collection." There also appears to be the necessary mental state because their conduct (breaking in and standing lookout) indicates an intent to follow through on their agreement (Application—Law to Fact Analysis).

2. Whether Mary and Monique committed larceny (Issue)

Both Mary and Monique may have committed the crime of larceny of the flashlight (Conclusion). Larceny is the trespassory taking without permission and carrying away of the personal property of another with the intent to deprive that person of it permanently (Rule).

In this case, Mary "stole" the flashlight, which satisfies the requirement that it be taken and carried away without permission. Further, the personal property was of another—in this instance, it belonged to the convenience store. The fact that she "stole" it also indicates that her mental state was to deprive the store of it permanently, meeting the second necessary element (Application—Law to Fact Analysis).

Monique may also be found guilty of the larceny as a co-conspirator. Under *Pinkerton v. United States*, a co-conspirator can be held vicariously liable for all crimes by other co-conspirators in furtherance of the conspiracy. "In furtherance of" means reasonably foreseeable (Application—Law to Fact Analysis).

In this case, it is reasonably foreseeable that to burglarize a home at night, some source of light will be necessary. (Application—Fact to Law Analysis). Thus, the larceny of the flashlight is in furtherance of the burglary and attributable to all co-conspirators, in this case Mary and Monique (Conclusion).

3. Burglary—Attempted burglary

a. Whether Monique or Mary committed burglary (Issue)

Mary and Monique probably did not commit burglary (Conclusion). Burglary at common law requires the breaking and entering of the dwelling house of another at night time with the intent to commit a felony therein (Rule). In this case, while it appears that Monique met the breaking and entering elements, as well as the requirement that the conduct occur at night, there was no dwelling house because the place Monique broke into and entered was a place used for computer storage, not as a dwelling (Application—Law to Fact Analysis).

b. Whether Mary and Monique committed attempted burglary (Issue)

Monique and Mary may have committed attempted burglary (Conclusion). Attempted burglary requires an overt act towards burglary that goes beyond mere preparation, accompanied by a mental state of an intent to commit burglary (Rule).

In this case, Monique actually broke into the house, which is an act far beyond mere preparation and certainly symbolic and manifest of an intent to commit burglary. When she broke in, she had the mental state of desiring to steal the art work, which constituted an intent to commit grand larceny, a felony (Application—Law to Fact Analysis). Accordingly, both elements appear to be met here. However, legal impossibility, as discussed in point 4 below, might be defense to their crime.

Mary could be held responsible for Monique's conduct either as a co-conspirator or an accomplice. Mary became an accomplice when she stood lookout in order to help Monique commit the crime of burglary, meeting both the actus reus of assisting the crime and the mental state requirement of intent.

4. Whether there us a valid defense of impossibility (Issue)

Monique and Mary may raise the defense of impossibility. Legal impossibility occurs when, had the act been completed, there would not have been a crime (Rule). Here, there was no dwelling house of another, so even if they had stolen the art work, it would not have been burglary (Application—Law to Fact Analysis). On the other hand, the prosecution will argue that this situation was factual impossibility, which is not a defense to an attempted crime (Alternative Analysis). Factual impossibility occurs when, because of an unforeseen factual or physical occurrence, the crime could not be completed (Rule). The unforeseen occurrence here is the use of the house for storage, and not as a dwelling. This case appears to fit the paradigm for factual impossibility because the act was dangerous and there was simply an unforeseen fact that technically prevents a conviction for burglary (Application—Law to Fact Analysis). Under these facts, it is unlikely that Mary and Monique would be successful in raising the defense of legal impossibility (Conclusion).

5. Whether Mary and Monique committed murder (Issue)

Murder is the unlawful killing of another human being with malice aforethought (Rule). In this case, there are different types of murder, including unintentional "depraved heart" murder and felony murder. Depraved heart murder requires a grossly reckless killing and felony murder is the killing of another human being during the commision of a felony or attempted felony. Monique did not intend to kill another human being, since the facts say she shot at a dog. Her actions, however, could be construed as grossly reckless, which would satisfy the requirements of gross reckless murder. She also killed another person (Fred), and her actions were the actual and proximate cause of Fred's death (Application—Law to Fact Analysis). If her actions were not considered grossly reckless, because she did not know that Fred was hiding out, she could also be found guilty of reckless/ negligent manslaughter (Conclusion). Furthermore, if Monique was considered to be in the process of committing a dangerous felony, attempted burglary, she met the requirements of felony murder by killing a human being (Fred, not the dog), during the commission of a felony. Under the felony murder rule, no intent to kill is required and co-felons Mary and Monique may be found guilty of felony murder.

Monique would not be able to claim self-defense regarding Fred's death because, first, she was defending against a dog, not a person and second, having broken into another's house, she was the aggressor and not an innocent person under attack. There appears to be no alternative defense available. Since the killing occurred during and in furtherance of the crime of attempted burglary, Mary also would be responsible for Fred's death under the co-conspirator rule imposing vicarious liability.

Question 2 (30 minutes)

Jake and Sarah were working in their barn in the twilight when a neighbor, Barry Bones, stopped by to visit. Barry, a large man who was known in the area as a bully, appeared to be drunk. Barry claimed Jake owed him money. A heated argument ensued. Barry said he'd be right back to "make Jake pay." When Barry returned, he had in his hand what appeared to be a .38 caliber handgun. He said, "You'd better give me the money, Jake; I don't want to humiliate you in front of Sarah." When Barry appeared to raise the gun toward the roof of the barn, Jake backed up toward the rear door of the barn. Suddenly, Sarah yelled, "Watch out, Jake! Kill him now!" Jake took out his own handgun and fired. The bullet killed Barry instantly. When Jake looked carefully at Barry's gun, it turned out to be a toy.

What crimes, if any, have Jake and Sarah committed?

Answer

1. Whether there was a solicitation to commit murder (Issue)

Sarah is likely guilty of solicitation to commit murder (Conclusion). Solicitation requires the act of enticing, encouraging, aiding, abetting, or facilitating a crime, in this case murder (Rule). The mental state required is intent, meaning purposely or knowingly asking, enticing, encouraging . . . another to commit murder. Here, Sarah encouraged Jake to shoot Bones, with the apparent intention that Jake do so (no joking here).

2. Whether the crime of murder was committed (Issue)

Jake, as well as Sarah in her capacity as an aider and abetter, may be guilty of the murder of Bones. Murder is the unlawful killing of another human being with malice aforethought. Jake shot Bones, actually and proximately causing Bones's death. While Jake's mental state is not exactly clear, it appears that Sarah's comment "Kill him now . . . ," coupled with the fact that Bones had raised his own gun, indicates that Jake shot Bones either intending to do him serious bodily harm or to kill him.

3. Whether Jake may claim self-defense (Issue)

Jake may claim self-defense. Self-defense may be raised when a person acts under the actual and reasonable belief of the need to repel imminent force likely to cause harm. Here, Jake, through no fault of his own, actually and reasonably believed that he was facing imminent serious bodily harm or death, or that his wife faced the same (which would also qualify under a defense of others). The fact that Bones's gun was a toy indicates that Jake made a mistake. If Jake's mistake was both honest and reasonable, he can still rely on self-defense. Given Bones's threat and overall demeanor, and the fact that the gun appeared to be real, Jake probably can claim self-defense.

CIVIL PROCEDURE EXAM QUESTION AND SAMPLE ANSWER

Question

Minnie Sota was born and raised in Delaware. For the past ten years, however, Minnie has driven a mobile home throughout the country. On her way from Minnesota, where she had parked the mobile home for the prior two years, to San Jose, California, to stay with her brother, Charlie, for a few years, Minnie stopped for gas in Reno, Nevada.

As she was exiting the freeway, Minnie spotted "Bob's Hot Tunes, Incorporated," a Delaware corporation. She purchased a new car stereo, filled her mobile home with gas, had a few drinks at a local bar, and then went on her way toward San Jose, California. As she approached San Jose, one of the knobs on Minnie's new car stereo sprang from the stereo and flew into her left eye. As a result, she swerved her car into the "Paramount Great America" sign on Route 101 in California. Minnie's mobile home was destroyed and Minnie comes to you seeking legal advice. After listening to her story, you find out that the knobs on her car stereo were defectively manufactured by Knobs Inc. Knobs Inc. is a Delaware corporation with its principal place of business in New York. It has shipped knobs exclusively to Bob's Hot Tunes for the past two years. You also find a federal statute that says, "It shall be a crime to sell defective knobs across state lines."

Should you file an action on Minnie's behalf in Federal District Court for the Northern District of California?

Answer

The first issue is whether it would be a Rule 11 violation to file a complaint on behalf of Minnie. Rule 11 requires that any paper filed in federal court be brought for a proper purpose and be warranted by law and fact. In this case, there is no evidence of improper purpose; Minnie has suffered injury and seeks compensation. Nor is the claim against Bob's or Knobs lacking in a legal or factual basis. Based on the facts, Minnie may state tort claims against Bob's and Knobs, both of whom may have breached a duty owed to Minnie which caused her injuries. Therefore, it would not be a Rule 11 violation to file those claims.

The second issue is whether the federal courts have subject matter jurisdiction over Minnie's claims. Federal courts are courts of limited jurisdiction. There must be a jurisdictional basis for each claim filed in federal court.

There are two primary bases for federal jurisdiction: (1) arising under, or (2) diversity. A claim arises under federal law if it is created by federal law. In this case, a federal statute makes it a crime to sell defective knobs across state lines. Assuming that the statute creates a course of action for a victim of defective knobs sold across state lines, this federal statute creates a course of action against Knobs, and therefore Minnie's claim against Knobs arises under federal law. Tort claims against the defendants, however, are created by state law and would not arise under federal law.

Even if the claims do not arise under federal law, there would still be federal jurisdiction if there is diversity. In order for there to be diversity jurisdiction, there must be complete diversity of citizenship and the amount in controversy must exceed $50,000.00. Citizenship means domicile, which means a person's true home, and where they intend to remain or to return. In this case, Minnie's domicile is Delaware because, although she traveled extensively in a mobile home and intends to stay in California for two years, she has evidenced no intent to establish a new permanent home in California or any other state. Accordingly, her domicile is Delaware, where she was born and raised. As a corporation, Bob's has dual citizenship. It is a Delaware corporation with its principal place of business in Reno, Nevada. Because Bob's is a Delaware corporation and because Minnie is a Delaware domiciliary, there is no complete diversity in this case. As between Minnie and Knobs, a Delaware corporation with its principle place of business in New York, there is diversity. If Knobs were sued without Bob's, there would be complete diversity. Moreover, the amount in controversy, the value of the mobile home, exceeds $50,000.00. Accordingly, there would be no subject matter jurisdiction over Minnie's claims against Bob's, but arising under and diversity jurisdiction are Minnie's claims against Knobs maintaining that action.

The third issue is whether the federal court in California has personal jurisdiction over the defendants. Personal jurisdiction is the power of the California court over the defendant's person or property. There is personal jurisdiction if the defendants consent to personal jurisdiction, if they are "present" in California, or if they engaged in such minimum contacts that it would not offend traditional notions of fair play and substantial justice to make them come to California to defend their action. In this case, there is no evidence that the defendants have consented to personal jurisdiction. Nor is there any evidence that they are present in California. As corporations, they are neither physically present in California, nor are they domiciled there. Moreover, there is no evidence that they engage in regular, continuous, or ongoing business in California.

Bob's, however, has such minimum contacts with California that it would not offend traditional notions of fair play and substantial justice to make it come to California to defend. Bob's has purposefully availed itself of California benefits. It is located on an off-ramp on an expressway close to California. It is in the business of installing stereos in mobile vehicles; thus it could, with significant previous experience, reasonably anticipate being called into California federal court. Nor will it be unduly burdensome to make it come from Reno to California to defend. The accident occurred in California, the plaintiff has an interest in having it resolved there, as does the state of California. Therefore, it would not be unconstitutional for the California federal court to assert personal jurisdiction over Bob's.

Knobs, however, has no direct ties, contacts, or relations with California. The question is, if by shipping components of a car stereo to a car stereo store located close to California, Knobs has purposefully availed itself of California and could reasonably anticipate being haled into court there. Absent any evidence of a track record of component parts entering California or causing injury there, Knobs could not foresee that it would litigate in California. Instead, its product entered California by the unilateral act of the plaintiff driving it there. Moreover, it would be burdensome for Knobs, a Delaware corporation with its principal place of business in New York, to travel to California to defend this action.

Accordingly, although the plaintiff's interest in suing Knobs together with Bob's in California is strong and the state's interest and the system's interest in the resolution of this case in one forum in California is also strong, those interests are outweighed by the absence of minimum contacts between Knobs and California. Therefore, it would be unconstitutional for California to assert personal jurisdiction over Knobs.

While the federal courts have subject-matter jurisdiction over Minnie's claim against Knobs, the California federal court has no personal jurisdiction over Knobs. Conversely, while the California courts have personal jurisdiction over Bob's, the federal courts have no subject-matter jurisdiction over Minnie's claim against Bob's. Therefore, I should not file this action in federal court in the Northern District of California.

SUCCESS ON EXAMS

- Organization and time allocation are everything: allocate 25 to 50 percent of your time to organization and to preparing your answer.

- You take the professor, not the course. Review past exams on file, class hypotheticals, and your professor's writings on the course topic area.

- Know the rules of law so that you can spot issues in fact patterns easily.

- Knowing the rules is not enough. You need to be able to analyze (apply the law to the facts) as well.

- Remember the three most important words in exam taking: In this case, . . .

- Read the question carefully and answer the question that is being asked.

- Write on one side of the page, skip lines, and use new paragraphs often in your responses.

- If you run out of time, outline your answer. Never write "Ran out of time." You certainly won't get any credit for this and you may even have a few points deducted for failure to allocate your time properly.

- The use of case names is not necessary. Know and identify the point of the case.

- Don't assume the professor knows what you are talking about. Be clear and address your points fully.

- Don't write your name on the exam blue book. Exams are graded anonymously. Violation of this will probably constitute an honor code violation and you may find yourself in the dean's office having some explaining to do.

- Be well rested for exams, and dress comfortably (be prepared for all room temperatures). Show up early for the exam (but not too early) and be ready to go. Have several sharpened pencils or pens.

- Leave as soon as you have completed the exam. The after-exam dialogue will only drive you crazy.

AFTER EXAMINATIONS: GRADES

If there is one thing that causes tension and division among law students, it's grades. Perhaps this is because they strongly influence your job prospects and determine who makes the prestigious "law review." Whatever the reason, students seem to lose all sense of reason when it comes to grades. However, you should not lose sight of the fact that the feedback you get through grades is minimal. Higher grades do not mean you will be a better lawyer than someone who earned lower grades. A final exam grade is just that—the evaluation of how you performed on that particular exam at that time. Your grade is important, but you should not confuse personal value and self-esteem with test performance, whether your performance is good or bad.

After the first set of exams, students sometimes create their own hierarchy based on how well other students are known or perceived to have fared. Schools don't help matters by ranking classes and giving honor distinctions and awards for excellence in test performance. By its very nature, the grading system is a cruel beast.

We have already mentioned that grading in law school tends to be harsher than in college. Students who routinely earned As and Bs in college may find themselves being awarded Bs and Cs in law school. Make the adjustment, and remember that most students will be having to do the same.

Class Rank

More important, perhaps, than the raw grade-point average is your class rank, that is, where you rank in relation to the rest of your class. Class rank is often a determining factor for eligibility on the school's student-published journal or law review, and is important to the hiring decisions of the larger law firms. Many law firms establish minimum levels of grade-point averages and class rank before they interview students on campus. Keep in mind, however, that these large firms represent only about 17 percent of the marketplace. The vast majority of jobs do not have such requirements.

Perhaps the most important employment opportunity that comes from high grades and class rank is the judicial clerkship. In the spring of the second year of school, you can apply for a clerkship with a federal judge, to commence after the student graduates. (You can apply for state court clerkships as well; these are also competitive and require high grades or other distinctions.)

Exam Reviews

Once you receive your grades, your professors may give you the opportunity to review your exams. This exercise may be far more important to you and your future success on law school exams than the grade itself: you need to understand *why* you got a particular grade.

Sometimes professors discuss the exam and the answers with the entire class. This is done because many students who initially wanted exam reviews may no longer need a private session after receiving a general explanation. It is advisable to attend the general review and to request a private session. Sometimes students find that their answers reflect what the professor seemed to be looking for more than their grade demonstrates. Bringing potential mistakes in grading to a professor's attention can only be done in a private exam review. Professors do make mistakes; they have many exams to grade.

CHAPTER 5

The Second Year of Law School

The second year of law school often differs dramatically from the first. You've passed what in many ways is the toughest year; you're familiar with the law and the casebooks. You're more in control. You can confidently handle longer reading assignments by briefing cases right in your text. You're less stressed in class. When the professor peers at you over his glasses and asks you a question, you may even find yourself thinking, "Oh, here we go again."

Perhaps the greatest difference between the first and second years, however, is the increased freedom of choice. For the most part, second-year students can choose the subject matter of their classes, and even the particular section of a class they wish to take. Of course, this flexibility does not mean that the second year is any easier than the first in terms of workload. In fact, now that you have the hang of it, professors are wont to hand you a lot more work. The second year is also when you should get involved in moot court competitions, law review and other journals, bar associations, mock trial—the list goes on and on. Many students also secure part-time jobs with law firms, and these are often high pressure. All this means, of course, that time management is equally important in the second year.

> Most students get legal jobs, outside, in the real world, during the academic year. Therefore, University of Maine Law School students are "big time" experienced before they even graduate. All students can find the courthouse and most can give a cogent legal argument in front of a judge by graduation."
>
> —*2L, University of Maine*

CLASSES AND CURRICULUM

The classroom experience often changes considerably after the first year. You will no longer be taking each course with the same group of students. Rather, your classes will include a mix of second- and third-year students, many of whom are already involved in professional life as law clerks and participating in extracurricular activities such as the law review or moot court.

Class discussion in the second year can tend towards imbalance, with a small group of students speaking most of the time. The depth of class discussion tends to go in two directions: deeper, because students have a broader and more meaningful knowledge base from which to speak, and nowhere, because those who get very involved in outside activities come to class less prepared. The latter group is making a grave mistake: they will be left in prayer at exam time, hoping they can pick up the material in the clutch. Remember that knowing the substantive background of a course is assumed, but by itself is not sufficient. You need to be able to work with that material on the exam.

Curriculum Choices

Few courses are required after the first year of law school; you are generally free to choose the areas of law you wish to study. Remember that a law degree is still the first or introductory level of legal education. You should consider exploring many areas of law as you examine your likes and dislikes. You might also focus on a particular area of law if you choose. You may select your courses according to the following criteria:

Subject Matter

Students wishing to practice in a particular field of the law can now focus on courses in their chosen area. For example, if you choose to specialize in taxation, you would include basic tax, partnership tax, corporate tax, etc., among your courses. If your school does not offer many courses in your chosen area, you may need to do independent work with a professor, take continuing legal education courses offered by the bar association, or take a course at another school.

Theory versus Practice

In the second year of law school, courses can be divided into theory-based and skills-based categories. Jurisprudence, for example, discusses legal theory. Theoretical courses generally focus on legal principles, the history of legal philosophy, and legal argument, whereas skills or clinical courses look at aspects like interviewing, negotiating, and trial or appellate advocacy. Clinic, on the other hand, offers practical experience under the supervision of a faculty member or adjunct professor.

Some schools have special programs which allow students to practice their skills with real clients and actual pending cases under the supervision of a trained law school clinician or professor. These programs are highly rewarding, especially if you are able to enroll in a program in which you are interested. In addition, such programs allow you to meet practitioners who may assist you later in your search for full-time work. Even if these connections prove useless, having some practical experience on your resume will always be advantageous in the job market.

Faculty members often disagree on the subject of the necessity for taking skills-based courses. We think it makes a lot of sense to gain as much practical experience as possible while still in school. Far from forsaking theory, skills courses often teach students how to apply it. Moreover, because American law schools, unlike those in other countries, do not require some form of apprenticeship, students would be wise to seek out clinical experience.

This seems to me to be a school where the focus is on a high level of training and cutting-edge theory in the basic subjects of the law. You can't spend three years here taking 'the easy' classes. Prepares you well for both academics and practice."

—*1L, University of Chicago*

The Bar Exam

Students often choose courses based on whether or not the subject matter will be on the Multistate Bar Examination. For example, commercial paper, wills and trusts, and securities law are all optional subjects that will most likely be tested on the bar. Of course, the bar exam tests important areas of the law, so you will undoubtedly benefit by taking courses on these subjects. However, think twice before taking a course solely to learn material for the bar, because if you take a bar review course prior to the exam, you can count on being taught the fundamentals of a particular area of law. Are we suggesting that you skip any of these important classes? Not necessarily. But don't hesitate to take those classes in which you have a genuine interest, and then take a review course to finish your preparation for the bar.

When the Course Is Offered

Some students refuse to take classes at 8:00 a.m. Others abhor evening classes. Still other students want classes bunched together over three days of the week so they can accommodate their work schedule (and others may just want long weekends). These considerations shouldn't be high on your list of priorities, but they are facts of life. After all, if you can't function at 8:00 a.m., then you might be better off taking a later class in which you can concentrate. Another consideration is that many school catalogs do not provide full course information. Some courses are not offered every year, while some courses are only offered during a particular semester. Moreover, many students may get closed out of the courses even when they are offered. The likelihood of getting closed out of a class should therefore be taken into account when you are selecting your course of study.

Final Exam Schedule

If taking a particular course creates an unreasonable final exam schedule, you should consider putting it off until you can avoid this problem. Academic deans do their best to avoid scheduling conflicts for students who are likely to take a particular track of classes, but it's not always possible to do so. Some schools adjust a student's final exam schedule if tests are within twenty-four or forty-eight hours of each other, so be sure to check with your school. Remember: the final exam is your grade, so monitor your exam schedule to keep it manageable.

THE TWO-YEAR MASTER PLAN

You can bet on one thing: you won't have the time in law school (at least before graduation) to take all the classes you would like to take. This means scheduling and planning are very important, and you should consider planning two years ahead rather than one semester at a time. The main reason for this is so you don't find yourself in the final semester with more required courses than you can handle. Keep in mind that a good lawyer is a good planner, so you might as well start now. And remember, you are not obligated to take all the courses you have included in your plan. As you take different courses, your interests and preferences may change.

Master Plan Considerations

Requirements/Basics
The fall of the second year of school is a good time to take some upper-level requirements. These include evidence, tax, corporations, wills and trusts, and professional responsibility. In some schools, this also includes constitutional law (where it's not required in the first year).

Skills Courses
You might choose a skills course to complement your regular theoretical/analytical courses. Skills courses include interviewing, counseling and negotiation, pre-trial litigation, trial advocacy, advanced legal writing, and specialized litigation courses such as family law litigation workshops. Some professors downplay the value of skill courses, believing them to be of less value than substantive courses, and holding the opinion that lawyers should gain experience once in practice. We feel, however, that law schools need to make a better effort to train their students in the art and skills of lawyering. It is therefore our opinion that you should use your time in law school to get an edge on skills training.

Prerequisites
You may choose a course because it is a prerequisite for a course you want to take later in your law school career. This is especially important if you plan on taking a clinic or externship, because usually these have significant requirements. For instance, many D.A. offices and the U.S. Attorney's office require that an extern complete both civil and criminal procedure before participating in their programs.

Mix and Match
You may want to consider selecting courses that have different requirements. Instead of taking four large classes worth three or four credit hours, why not take a seminar with a paper requirement as well? Or how about a skills course such as pre-trial litigation that is concluded by the last day of classes? In this way, you reduce the pressure of finals by taking other valuable courses which do not have a final examination requirement.

Other Parameters

Choosing courses in the fall of the second year may be easier than other upper-level semesters because there are so many choices. On the other hand, be judicious in selecting classes. If you get closed out of a few courses that interest you, start basing your decisions on different parameters. A good finals schedule and having large blocks of time in which to study or involve yourself in extracurricular activities might be worthy considerations.

EXTRACURRICULAR ACTIVITIES

In the second year of law school you will find that, with a heavier workload, time is an even more precious commodity than it was in the first year. Nevertheless, don't make the mistake of avoiding extracurricular activities. Here are just a few reasons why you should find time for activities outside the classroom:

- Comraderie with colleagues
- An opportunity to stay within the realm of law but get out of the classroom
- A chance to develop skills
- A forum in which to build connections
- Increasing resume value

Extracurricular activities are meant to be fun and educational. Here are some of your options:

Moot Court

In moot court, students receive a hypothetical case scenario based in an area of law which has already been addressed in an actual court of law. It is the student's responsibility to analyze the facts and legal issues in order to complete an appellate brief. The student is also responsible for developing an oral argument for both sides of the issue. Moot court takes place in competitions at the school, regional, national, and multi-national levels. The competitions are scored based on writing ability and oral argument skills.

The teams for an interscholastic competition are often selected through a tryout process hosted by a moot court board, which usually consists of succssful second- or third-year law students. Faculty members in charge of the program may participate in the selections as well. Selection for a team can be based on G.P.A., writing skills, related college or life experience, or even a sample argument taken from a tryout problem. Competitors are usually given six weeks to three months to complete the brief and additional time in which to prepare oral arguments. Winning an award in moot court can be a strong addition to your resume.

Students who meet grade requirements or who are successful in competitions are usually eligible to apply for the Moot Court Board. These boards organize tryouts and events and may host regional or national competitions. Students who are elected to the boards often receive credit hours and/or scholarships for their participation.

Here is a short list of moot court competitions:

ADMINISTRATIVE LAW

> University of Dayton School of Law
> National Administrative Law Moot Court Competition

AFRICAN-AMERICAN ISSUES

> National Black Law Students Association
> Frederick Douglass Moot Court Competition

BANKRUPTCY

> American Bankruptcy Institute, St. John's University School of Law
> Judge Conrad B. Duberstein Moot Court Competition

CIVIL RIGHTS

> University of Minnesota Law School
> Civil Rights Moot Court Competition

CLIENT COUNSELING

> American Bar Association Law Student Division
> Young Lawyers Division Client Counseling Competition

CONSTITUTIONAL LAW

Holderness Moot Court, University of North Carolina
Law School

J. Braxton Craven, Jr., Memorial Moot Court
Competition, American University

Washington College of Law

Burton D. Wechsler First Amendment Moot Court
Competition, University of Wisconsin Law School

Evan A. Evans Constitutional Law Moot Court
Competition

American College of Trial Lawyers and the Bar of
the City of New York

National Moot Court Competition

The Moot Court Board of the Marshall-Wythe School
of Law

College of William and Mary and the Virginia Trial
Lawyers Association

William B. Spong Invitational Moot Court Competition
Columbus School of Law, Catholic University of
America

Sutherland Cup

CORPORATE LAW

Widener University School of Law

Ruby R. Vale Interschool Corporate Moot Court
Competition

CRIMINAL LAW

Canadian Bar Association-Ontario

Gale Cup Moot Court Competition

CRIMINAL PROCEDURE

Seton Hall University Law School, Seton Hall
University Law

School Alumni Association Inn of Court

John J. Gibbons National Criminal Procedure
Competition

University of San Diego School of Law
National Criminal Procedure Competition

ENTERTAINMENT AND COMMUNICATIONS LAW

Benjamin N. Cardozo School of Law, Cardozo-BMI Entertainment and Communications Law Moot Court Competition

ENVIRONMENTAL LAW

Ohio Valley National Resource and Environmental Law Center

Salmon P. Chase College of Law, Northern Kentucky University

Chase National Environmental Law Competition

Pace University School of Law

National Environmental Law Moot Court Competition

EVIDENCE LAW

Brooklyn Law School

Jerome Prince Invitational Evidence Competition

FAMILY LAW

Albany Law School of Union University

Judge Domenick L. Gabrielli, New York Court of Appeals (Retired)

Domenick L. Gabrielli National Family Law Competition

GENERAL

The Shepard Broad Law Center at Nova University
F. Lee Bailey Moot Court Competition

American Bar Association, Law Students Division, Young Lawyers Division, Section of Litigation; the Appellate Judges' Conference of the ABA through the Fund for Justice and Education National Appellate Advocacy Competition

The Association of the Bar of the City of New York

American College of Trial Lawyers National Moot
Court Competition

HEALTH LAW

Southern Illinois University School of Law

S.I.U. School of Medicine, Department of Medical
Humanities, and the American College of Legal
Medicine

National Health Law Moot Court Competition

INSURANCE LAW

Insurance Institute of the University of Connecticut
BAR/BRI, and Lexis-Nexis Inc.

William F. Starr Insurance Law Competition

INTELLECTUAL PROPERTY LAW

American Intellectual Property Law Association

Giles Sutherland Rich Moot Court Competition

INTERNATIONAL LAW

International Law Students Association, Mead Data
Central, Inc. /Lexis, ABA Section of Litigation

Philip C. Jessup International Law Moot Court
Competition

Canada-United States Law Institute

Niagara Cup International Moot Court Competition

LABOR LAW

New York Law School

Robert F. Wagner, Sr., National Labor Law Moot Court
Competition

LAW AND ECONOMICS

George Mason University School of Law and Economics
Moot Court Competition

MEDICAL-LEGAL ETHICS

Allen Siegel, Esquire, and Duke Law School

Rabbi Seymour Siegel Moot Court Competition

NATIONAL SECURITY LAW
George Washington University
National Security Law Moot Court Competition

NEGOTIATION
American Bar Association, Law Student Division, Young Lawyers Division
Negotiation Competition

INFORMATION TECHNOLOGY and PRIVACY LAW
The John Marshall Law School
National Moot Court Competition in Information Technology and Privacy Law

PRODUCTS LIABILITY
University of Cincinnati College of Law
Rendigs, Fry, Kiely and Dennis, August A. Rendigs, Jr., National Products Liability Competition

SECURITIES LAW
Fordham University School of Law
Irving R. Kaufman Memorial Moot Court Competition

SPACE LAW
Association of U.S. Members of the International Institute of Space Law (AUSMIISL) and the International Institute of Space Law
International Institute of Space Law Moot Court Competition

SPORTS LAW
Tulane Law School
Tulane Mardi Gras Invitational

TAX LAW
State University of New York at Buffalo Law School
Albert R. Mugel National Tax Competition
Florida Bar, Tax Section
National Tax Moot Court Competition

TELECOMMUNICATIONS LAW

Federal Communications Bar Association, J. Columbus School of Law

National Telecommunications Competition

TRADEMARK AND UNFAIR COMPETITION

Brand Names Education Foundation

Saul Lefkowitz National Moot Court Competition

Mock Trial

Mock trials are similar to moot court in that they are a fun learning experience. In a mock trial arena, the student prepares the case at the trial court level. So, in a mock trial competition the student is responsible for preparing witnesses, opening and closing arguments, direct and cross-examination, and for gathering together the trial documents and exhibits. Students at many schools have the opportunity to participate in mock trial scenarios by enrolling in trial advocacy courses. Students who wish to compete outside the school usually have to pass before a panel of professors who serve as team advisors. Credit hours are almost always earned for team participation, and mock trial offers substantive skills training. In many competitions, there are even cash awards for success.

Here is a short list of trial advocacy competitions:

National Association of Criminal Defense Lawyers

Cathy Bennett National Criminal Trial Competition

Academy of Trial Lawyers of Allegheny County

Gourley Moot Court Competition

The John Marshall Law School, ABA Criminal Justice Section

National Criminal Justice Trial Advocacy Competition

Texas Young Lawyers Association

National Mock Trial Competition

Association of Trial Lawyers of America

National Student Trial Advocacy Competition

Some resources on trial advocacy:

Bergman, Paul. Trial Advocacy in a Nutshell. *St. Paul, MN: West Publishing Company.*

Jeans, James. Trial Advocacy. *St. Paul, MN: West Publishing Company.*

Lisnek, Paul M. and Eric Oliver. The Complete Litigator: Reality and Perception in and out of the Courtroom. *Andrews Publications, 1994. (800-847-7285)*

McElhaney, James. Trial Notebook: A Practical Primer on Trial Advocacy. *Chicago: American Bar Association. (312-988-5000)*

"Special opportunities, like tutoring a first-year class, being a research assistant on a Supreme Court brief, performing in the annual 'Libel and Slander' show, and participating in several student groups have made my time here rewarding beyond my highest expectations!"
— *1L, Duquesne*

Law Reviews or Other Journals and Publications

Law reviews are student-run organizations that generally accept material based on G.P.A. Students who are in the top 10 or 15 percent of their class normally qualify for law review. Once they have qualified, they must write an article over the course of one semester. The completed article is reviewed by members of the law review editorial board, which consists of upperclassmen who successfully completed the program and were elected to replace the previous board. The board then either accepts, rejects, or conditionally accepts the article.

The board is responsible for publishing a yearly series of articles written by practitioners, judges, academics, and students. The board is required to solicit, review, and edit articles for publication.

Law review members also receive credit hours and/or scholarships at many schools. In addition, employers have a high regard for law review when hiring because of the grade requirements and writing skills necessary for acceptance.

There are other opportunities besides the law review for students to get published. First, students who do not pass the law review board's requirements may still submit an article to the board for consideration. Authors of articles which are chosen in this way are invited to be on the law review. Second, many campuses have other journals which accept writing about specific areas of law, and there is usually no grade requirement. The legal community has a great deal of respect for these publications; in fact, you might find that more practicing lawyers read these journals (in health, tax, or international law, for example) than law reviews. So, if your grades don't get you on the law review, fear not. There are still plenty of places you can publish your work.

Special Interest Groups

Special interest groups like the International Law Society and Intellectual Property Club focus on a particular area of the law. Clubs like these often participate in charity drives or other charitable events in their local communities. They also host regular meetings at which practitioners in the field speak, and attend events related to their interest. These clubs provide great opportunities to network with other students and professionals.

Human Interest Organizations

Law student groups such as the Black Law Students Association, Decalogue Society, Gay and Lesbian Students, and Asian Law Students Association, provide opportunities for exploring areas of mutual concern to law students. These are also a great way to network and make friends with influential people. As above, these organizations are often involved with charity and other community work. In addition, they often host events with corresponding organizations at other law schools and affiliated national groups. Many of the national bodies also run special moot court competitions.

Academic Groups

Groups such as Phi Delta Phi or National Law Society are based on academic accomplishment. The Phi Delta Phi Law Fraternity is the largest and oldest international legal fraternity, with Inns in the United States, Canada, Mexico, and Guatemala. This fraternity requires high professional standards and good academic standing of its members. Inns often hold monthly meetings, organize charitable and community events, and sponsor lectures.

Common Purpose Groups

Groups like Phi Alpha Delta and the Student Bar Association are student-based organizations which sponsor social and charity events and get involved in school policy issues. The Phi Alpha Delta Law Fraternity is the largest professional law fraternity in the United States. It is made up of various different chapters which often aspire to service the school, the student, the profession, and the community. The individual chapters hold monthly meetings and organize charitable events such as food drives and blood drives. Membership in this fraternity is a nice way to meet and talk with other law students outside law school.

BAR ASSOCIATIONS

Join them and get involved! It's a shame that so few students join bar associations, because they are laden with networking opportunities. Bar associations are where you can meet the leading people in your field of interest. This may be one of the best-kept secrets when it comes to job searching.

Local Bar Associations

Students who join local bar associations can attend seminars and committee meetings. Doing so exposes them to practical aspects of local legal practices and informs them about current issues and developments in the law. Student members can also make important contacts with local practitioners. Local bar associations organize sports leagues and community service projects, offer subscriptions to journals or newsletters, and give discounts to conferences, seminars, and even at local restaurants and entertainment establishments, car rentals, health clubs, and the like. Students are also encouraged to participate in special student-oriented activities such as career seminars and programs to prepare them for the bar.

State Bar Association

Most state bar associations have a law-student division. Membership often provides law students with practical benefits such as subscriptions to journals and newsletters and notices about seminars and lectures sponsored by the association. Membership also enables students to meet practicing attorneys. In addition, such associations may offer sponsored insurance plans and discount programs.

American Bar Association

The American Bar Association has a law-student division which organizes activities for students throughout the year. Division members are eligible for appointment as liaisons to committees of the ABA and may also hold elected or appointed offices in national law-student divisions. Members are encouraged to participate in programs like the law-student division convention and local events with practicing attorneys, professors, and members of the bench. Members also receive a one-year subscription to both the ABA journal and the student lawyer magazine. As well, the ABA student division offers an insurance plan and membership to various ABA section groups.

CHAPTER 6

THE THIRD YEAR OF LAW SCHOOL

THE TRANSITION FROM SCHOOL TO PRACTICE

The third year of law school finds some students with "senioritis," an affliction characterized by symptoms such as an anxiousness to graduate, a carelessness about class preparation, and an urgency to see the "real world," that is, the world beyond law school. Sufferers may have been offered a job on graduation and feel that they have nothing more to prove academically. Or they might not yet have a job offer and are still unsure about their prospects after law school. Sufferers in the latter category are probably actively looking for an entry-level position with an appropriate firm or office and do not devote as much time to their studies as they should.

Senioritis, we shouldn't have to say, is better avoided. Whether or not you have a job lined up, you should keep your focus on your school work until graduation. Always keep in mind that grades may be important for subsequent graduate school applications, and that potential employers may question a weak showing in the final year.

"Law school is like the desert, except it is not quite as hot and you don't get sand in your shoes. Some people find their own oasis and live in paradise like a Bedouin prince. Others trudge on endlessly and finally collapse of heat exhaustion. Your best bet is to try to find a cactus every now and then and suck the juice out of it."
—*3L, Ohio State University*

SELECTING COURSES IN THE THIRD YEAR

If you already have a job offer, then you might want to take courses that will directly relate to your new position in order to develop skills your employer will appreciate. If you don't yet have a job offer, take courses that will develop your skills as a lawyer by expanding your potential areas of practice. In any event, you can use your last year of law school to take courses in areas that will be covered on the bar exam.

THE BAR EXAM

If you haven't found permanent employment before graduation, don't be surprised if law firms are reluctant to hire you until you pass the state's bar exam. Of course, preparing for the bar adds pressure to your already demanding academic schedule. But preparation for the bar exam is crucial, because good academic performance in law school does not guarantee a passing score.

Preparing for the Bar Exam

In almost every jurisdiction in the United States, passing the bar exam is required before a student is permitted to practice law and adopt the title "attorney." (In Wisconsin, you don't have to take a bar exam if you attend law school in the state and remain there to practice.) Over the last twenty years, bar exams have changed considerably, both to reflect the changing needs of the profession and to standardize the legal profession among the various states. For example, the Multistate Professional Responsibility Examination has been added for all prospective attorneys.

The bar exam focuses on the fundamentals of law, such as torts, contracts, criminal law, corporations, and wills and trusts. No matter how convinced you are that you will never practice, say, criminal law, you will still need a good understanding of the area in order to pass the bar exam.

Generally speaking, the exam does not test the so-called "specialties" such as intellectual property or entertainment law. Everyone in a particular state is required to take and pass the same bar examination, regardless of the area of law in which they intend to practice, and an additional exam must be taken in order to practice either patent or maritime law.

Many students forget the importance of learning the basics for the bar exam and focus their energies on the area in which they plan to practice. These students tend to rely on preparatory courses for the bar examination. Preparatory courses are usually offered during the last few months before the exam and cover areas of law that may be on the test. You should understand that while these courses are a good supplement to your school work, there is no substitute for a solid academic background. Material from as many as twenty-five law school courses may be covered on the exam. You need exposure to law courses which encourage your analytical abilities as well as those which provide at least a basic understanding of the "black letter" law and the established rules and principles of practice.

What to Expect on the Bar Examination

The bar exam is given twice a year: in February and July. In most states, it consists of two parts. One part is a day-long examination consisting of multiple-choice questions in general areas of practice (the Multistate Bar Examination or MBE). The second part consists of essay and multiple-choice questions which focus on the relevant state's significant areas of practice (the State Bar Examination).

The Multistate Bar Examination is the same in almost every state and is taken on the same day by everyone in the country. The MBE is a multiple-choice exam lasting one day and tests your ability to handle the fundamentals of legal practice. These fundamentals include questions on property, contracts, torts, constitutional law, criminal law, and commercial transactions.

The MBE is difficult for most students simply because of the sheer quantity of material covered. It consists of two hundred questions in one day-long examination (less than two minutes per question). This may appear manageable to students used to taking multiple-choice examinations in undergraduate classes or in law school. However, what makes the MBE especially difficult is that none of the questions are ever identified as "contracts," "torts," or "property." For instance, a question might appear to involve contract principles but then prove to be a question about real estate conveyances, and it may be followed up by a question with a similar fact pattern concerning entirely different legal issues.

The requirements for passing the MBE vary from state to state, depending on the emphasis placed on that portion of the exam by the relevant state bar authorities. In most states, however, it is possible to pass the MBE with as little as 65-70 percent of the questions answered correctly. You should not rely on this statistic, however, since passing the bar exam will depend more on your overall performance than on how well you do on either a given multistate or essay portion of the exam.

The second part of the bar exam (which may be given the first day of the exam in some states) is the state bar exam. This portion of the exam is usually composed of essay questions and is oriented to the nuances of the state in which the applicant intends to practice. In some states, such as New Jersey, this portion of the exam may consist of questions in only a few subject areas. In others, such as Illinois, as many as twenty subject areas may be tested on the essay portion of the exam.

Taking the Bar Exam

The bar exam effectively extends the school year by three months. Try to begin studying for it a few days after the last day of your finals. The bar exam is difficult in large part because it changes so often. However, it is not so difficult that anyone who took an appropriate balance of substantive courses shouldn't be able to pass it. It is a manageable task if you don't try to learn everything in the few weeks prior to the exam. The fact that many bar applicants take prep courses has a tendency to level the playing field and create a sense of unity among applicants.

Preparatory courses for the bar exam provide a good overview of the areas covered on the exam, and most students are well served by a review of the course work. The courses emphasize that it is not necessary to relearn every case and each rule of law. Rather, you should focus on the types of issues that are likely to be tested on the exam and what the bar examiners consider a passing answer.

As we said earlier, prep courses are by no means a replacement for good solid school work. They should be used to establish a positive mindset for approaching the exam. Establish a study schedule to ensure adequate time for each subject so you don't need to cram at the end. In the best of worlds, you will also be able to allow time for relaxation or general review on the few days before the examination. Schedule your study so that it is comfortable, not pressing.

On the day of the examination, arrive early. Have a good breakfast and don't cram at the last minute. You should aim to take the exam in the knowledge that you have prepared adequately. Once the exam is distributed, take time to look through the whole thing and allot an appropriate amount of time per question so you don't end up having to tackle a disproportionate number of questions in very little time. Read each question all the way through without drawing any conclusions. It may be helpful to read "the call of the question" prior to reading the fact pattern. As mentioned, bar exam essay questions are often ambiguous as to the area they are testing. A question may read as though it concerns corporations when actually it raises an agency issue. Therefore, you must read the entire question first. Next, take a few moments to draft an outline for your response, ensuring that you outline the issue, specify the rule of law, and apply the rule to the issue. Unlike many law school essays, your answers on the bar exam must be concise because the response space is limited.

When the first day of the exam is over, you would be well advised to spend the evening relaxing. You should not plan an evening of intense study, although you may wish to review briefly the basics before the next day's testing. It is important to be well rested and alert on each day of the bar exam.

CHAPTER 7

ENTERING PRACTICE

HAVING A SUCCESSFUL LEGAL CAREER

Beginning the practice of law is the culmination of countless hours of classes, exams, and pressure: in short, hard work. You've just passed the bar exam and the character and fitness examination process. You are ready to embark on your career as a lawyer. You might be wondering if, after all, you've made the right decision. Is this the field and the job for which you are really suited?

Consider the following statement from Deborah Arron's *Running from the Law:* "As startling as it may sound, more than four attorneys out of every ten have expressed a desire to work at something other than law." Arron's data were taken from a study by Smith College, published in the *ABA Journal* in February 1984. Arron reviewed the statistics and concluded that the years following law school are often characterized by high levels of dissatisfaction.

Certainly, practicing law is not for everyone, and unfortunately some people don't realize this until after they've passed the bar exam. This is why undertaking some personal research into the matter and doing things like taking law school preparation courses is strongly recommended before committing to law school.

If you're feeling unsure about your career choice as you enter the practice of law, don't despair too early. Always be clear about your priorities and keep them in mind. Concentrate on the goals you've set, but take the time to monitor your interests as you go. The opportunities available to lawyers today are as diverse as the population itself. Countless human undertakings require legal counsel, and it's always possible to steer yourself towards those which interest you most. Some people walk away from a position in a law firm or corporate environment to work as a talent agent, business manager, or entrepreneur. Clearly, a law degree brings value to any walk of life. So, if a career outside a traditional arena is what you desire, then go for it.

> *I believe that law school is a great education for anyone, even if there are too many lawyers. I think it teaches critical thinking, which is important for an individual's growth, as well as being beneficial to society."*
>
> — *3L, Widener*

On the other hand, many people are, of course, happy to follow a more conventional occupation as an attorney. If this is the case, the following are some of the environments in which you might choose to work.

WORK ENVIRONMENTS

Law Firm/Private Practice

A law firm or private practice is a group of lawyers joined in a partnership. As business grows, other lawyers are hired as associates, and they may eventually become members of the partnership. Large firms are often "full service" entities, meaning they handle a wide range of legal issues. They generally offer high starting salaries, but lawyers in these firms often find themselves working seven days a week, from early in the morning to late in the evening. Some lawyers thrive on this pressure, others merely tolerate the experience until their school loans are paid off. Medium-sized firms tend to concentrate their practice in a few specific areas of the law. For example, a firm might focus on defending insurance policy holders who are being sued for alleged negligence. Because of their smaller size, these firms tend to pay somewhat smaller salaries. One benefit, however, of working for a smaller firm is that it is generally easier to obtain a partnership; there are simply fewer people working their way to the top.

Government

Many new lawyers concentrate on either civil or criminal work as public defenders, district attorneys, or some other position in government. Starting salaries are usually low in this environment, but one is often given the opportunity to enter the courtroom right away. In private practice it can be years before you are permitted to handle a jury trial, since most clients prefer such matters to be handled by the senior lawyers. Some lawyers begin in government practice in order to obtain trial experience before moving on to the private sector.

Corporation

A few large corporations hire new law graduates, although most prefer seasoned lawyers. Lawyers in this environment manage litigation, often with outside lawyers and firms, so it is helpful to have some real-world experience. Many lawyers find a shift to the corporate environment a nice change in lifestyle. A stable salary with bonuses can add up to a comfortable compensation package.

Education

The best and brightest law students generally have the opportunity to become law school professors, although there is definitely some value in practicing law for a few years before stepping into the classroom. Law students seem to distinguish between professors who are able to ground their teaching in the real world and those who have never practiced law. Teaching at a law school is very prestigious, so competition is stiff; only those students who graduate at the top of their class are candidates for teaching positions.

Judicial Clerkship

Many top students are offered the opportunity to clerk for an appellate or Supreme Court justice. These few fortunate students perform research and assist in the drafting of judicial decisions. Needless to say, a great deal of prestige is attached to these positions. In some cases, large law firms are willing to extend an offer of employment for a year or two to permit the candidate the chance to accept a clerkship. The law firm can then boast of the former judicial clerk's credentials when it comes to swaying potential clients.

AREAS OF PRACTICE

Whatever work environment you ultimately select, you will also need to consider the particular substantive areas of law in which you will practice. Here are some of the more popular areas.

Personal Injury and Insurance Defense Litigation

When someone is injured because of the possible negligence or alleged wrongdoing of another, a tort action may arise. In such a lawsuit, the injured party sues another party for money or other compensation for damages. Many attorneys make careers out of representing one side or the other in personal injury litigation. Defense attorneys working for insurance companies and private enterprises have fairly stable hours. Their job is not always to defeat the claims of an injured person, but to ensure that, if their client is liable for the injury, a payment is made which is commensurate with the damages. Attorneys who represent plaintiffs, on the other hand, represent individuals who often cannot afford the hourly rates of attorneys. These attorneys typically work on a contingency fee, receiving a percentage of the injured person's monetary recovery from a successful suit.

Family Law

Family lawyers concentrate on the legal concerns relevant to the interpersonal relationships between family members. Trusts, estates, prenuptial agreements, divorce, and child custody proceedings are some of the areas in which these attorneys practice. This field is challenging and quite strenuous, because it often requires moderating between people whose relationship has soured. Lawyers must work their clients through irrational and vengeful positions to seek resolution.

Tax Law

This area is dominated by lawyers who possess undergraduate or graduate degrees in accounting or finance in addition to their law degrees. Tax attorneys represent a range of clients, from impoverished individuals to large corporations. In each case, the lawyer represents her client's interests in a potential or pending dispute over the interpretation of tax law. Many lawyers also work for the IRS itself and prosecute cases which allege abuse or improper conduct by a taxpayer.

International Law

International lawyers are involved in disputes between governments and people of different countries. Fluency in a second language and the desire to travel are almost prerequisites. In addition, an employer will look for evidence that you understand the culture and people of a particular country, so contacts in that country are also important.

Intellectual Property

Although students must take a separate bar exam in order to practice patent law, there is no such requirement for those who wish to practice trademark or copyright law. Nevertheless, most copyright and trademark disputes are handled by patent lawyers, whose comprehensive understanding of the issues is beneficial. Patent law, in a nutshell, protects the rights of inventors and creators of their legally cognizable ideas. Copyright law protects the reproduction or publication of some matter and form (literary, musical, artistic, etc.). Trademark law also protects the brand names and marks of companies that have established their identities in particular business areas.

Criminal Law

Lawyers who prosecute criminals are generally employed by the government. Criminal defendants, that is, people accused of violating the law, are represented either by a lawyer in private practice or by a public defender. The Constitution provides everyone the right to representation by a lawyer when criminal charges are pending.

Labor Law

Hiring and firing practices, fair labor standards, the regulation of work environments and unions, as well as concerns such as the disposition of pension funds, are all the purview of labor lawyers. The work often requires them to argue the meaning of national labor laws in federal courts and to travel to the national offices of employers and union leaders. Again, labor lawyers may specialize in representing either the interests of companies or those of unions or employees.

Bankruptcy

Bankruptcy lawyers concentrate their efforts on defending or prosecuting parties in financial difficulty. A person who files for bankruptcy certainly needs legal assistance, but so do those people and entities with claims against that person (creditors, for example). The focus of this practice requires knowledge of the United States Bankruptcy Code, which contains atypical nuances and rules. Bankruptcy is an area full of technicalities in which it is difficult for attorneys with no course work or background to excel.

Real Estate

Real estate lawyers represent the interests of parties involved in the buying or selling of property or a conflict regarding property. The many responsibilities of a lawyer in this field include drafting and negotiating contracts and leases, reviewing sales agreements and mortage documents, and performing title searches.

Corporate Law

Running a business is a complex venture. Companies merge, make acquisitions, sign and dissolve contracts, etc. In short, companies are involved in numerous affairs controlled by local, state, and federal laws. Corporate lawyers guide companies through routine but labyrinthine legal processes and monitor and represent the interests of their clients.

Health Law

Health law is perhaps the fastest growing field of the law. It focuses on difficult issues such as adequate care for the elderly, AIDS research, legal obligations to patients, use of unapproved medicines, etc. The health care lawyer is always learning and keeping abreast of new scientific and political developments in the field, each day perhaps changing the position and case from what it was the day before.

Entertainment Law

Combining several areas of practice, including contracts and civil law, these lawyers interact with celebrities and sports figures. Perhaps people are just people, but the terms of a record or movie deal, the rights in one's image and work, or disputes between producers, directors, and actors, may all require legal representation. Too often, people unknowingly waive certain rights or interests simply because they don't know any better.

Public Interest

These positions are largely supported by non-profit organizations and private donations. Assisting people who are unable to assist themselves, public interest agencies attempt to meet the seemingly ever-increasing need to help the under-represented. Lawyer salaries are low, indeed, but perhaps no area of the law provides as much satisfaction as working for the public good. Many states and the American Bar Association often consider requiring all lawyers to devote a portion of their time to assisting those in need of legal services who otherwise could not afford them (pro bono). Until such requirements take effect, the under-represented will continue to be thankful for the lawyers who put the public good ahead of their own monetary welfare.

Course Outlines

INTRODUCTION AND DISCLAIMER

The appendix which follows presents three sample outlines. They are actual course outlines prepared by a law student while taking these courses. We share them with you, with former law student Sue Gordon's permission, because they illustrate what a course outline could look like. You may or may not choose to outline a course the same way, but it is often useful to see what someone else has done. Since Ms. Gordon achieved very high grades in her law school courses, we thought her approach would offer a good example.

Note: No claim is made as to the accuracy or content of the outlines. They are based on the particular casebooks and materials used in this student's course and the emphasis placed on the material by her law professors. Your courses may (and likely will) not duplicate these outlines. They *not* being provided for their accuracy or in any way as a substitute for actual course materials or study guides.With these considerations in mind, go on and check out the outlines that worked quite well for one very successful law student.

LEGAL METHOD

I. **MATERIALS AND METHODS OF LAW STUDY**
Two forms of law (case law and legislation)

A. CASE LAW

1. How Cases Make Law—Originates in decisions of judges or other officials empowered by constitution or laws to hear and decide particular controversies

2. Common Law Doctrine Of Precedent (Stare decisis)

   a. Originated in Eng., decisions in past shape future laws

   b. More flexible than statutes

   c. Cases of first impression—decision of court must proceed without prior judicial interpretations

   d. Advantages

      i. Flexibility, not bound by confines of precise language of statute, may be several ways to articulate same rule

      ii. Can reflect changing needs in society. Allows us to adapt to social change

      iii. Laws may be consistent over period of time, but inconsistent in long term

      iv. Can be more responsive if case comes before judge

      v. Statutory law has limitations in the use of language, will be ambiguous

3. Res Judicata, Stare Decisis, Reversal and Overruling—Stare Decisis, Doctrine of Precedent—not disturbing that which has been decided; places responsibility on judge to determine cases based on past decisions; courts permitted to depart from stare decisis; generally binding but not rigid; if follow stare at least

know what rule is; cases where facts are same; what weight does precedent have?

a. Binding authority—judge should follow

b. Persuasive authority—court can change

a. Binding Authority—decision from higher court is binding on lower court in same jurisdiction. Even if some time has gone by

b. If case determined by court in another jurisdiction of same level or higher, decision is persuasive authority. Not binding

DICTUM—only persuasive authority. Court addressing things not in facts or present in particular case — standard by means of which we can predict, under certain fact situations, a decision the court must consider holding

HOLDING—Fully authoritative and generally binding. Rule of law we can take away from case

REVERSAL—if trial judge does not follow precedent. On appeal, the appellate court will reverse decision of lower court in same controversy in order to follow precedent

OVERRULE—Court can only overrule its own precedent or something that once was precedent. Can not overrule precedent from higher court. Can only reverse or affirm current case. When court of last resort overrules decision, does not affect current controversy but decision is no longer authoritative precedent. Deviation from stare decisis

RES JUDICATA—When decision has been appealed as far as it can go or time limitation expires, the decision is final. Can be overruled for precedent but decision on that case is res judicata

PENDUS JURISDICTION—If state and federal issues in same case, fed. courts may hear and make decisions on all issues. However, fed. decision of state issue is not binding to state. Fed. ct. however can determine whether state law is constitutional

4. DECISIONS FROM OTHER JURISDICTIONS
If case determined by court in another jurisdiction, decision is only persuasive authority

5. ADMINISTRATIVE ADJUDICATION
Lawyers must work with "unconstrued legislation" (statutes, provisions never before subjected to judicial scrutiny/interpretation)

B. LEGISLATION, ATTRIBUTES AND TYPES

1. TYPES OF LEGISLATION
   a. Constitution—law of highest authoritativeness and obligation
      i. Article I, Section I—all legislative powers granted shall be vested in U.S. Congress
      ii. Section 8—Congress makes laws necessary and proper for carrying into Execution the foregoing powers
      iii. Article 6, P. 2—Supremacy Clause, judges in every state shall be bound to Constitution to the contrary notwithstanding
      iv. Article 2, Section 2—President has power to make treaties provided 2/3 Senate concurs
   b. Federal Administrative Regulations—Prescribed by Federal Agency; superior to authoritativeness of state law; rule-making process of Federal Agencies governed by Administrative Procedure Act
   c. State Constitutions—Easier to repeal/amend statute than to amend constitution; Supreme Court of U.S. not superior to state courts on questions of local state law

d. State Statutes—Important developments:
   i. Extension and intense development of state controls, e.g. consumer protection
   ii. Increasing tendency of state legislatures to intervene by replacing old case law rules with new legislative norms
e. State Administrative Legislations—State and local rule-making processes often informal and unstructured; many states adopted <u>Revised Model State Administrative Procedure Act</u>
f. Municipal Ordinances (by-laws)—rules of local legislative origin; usually supported by sanction of fine or penalty. Recent tendency to empower courts to formulate and prescribe rules governing procedures followed by litigants and judges in contested cases; Best known rules of court are <u>federal rules of civil procedure</u>

II. CASE LAW, ANALYSIS AND SYNTHESIS OF JUDICIAL DECISIONS

A. STATE AND FEDERAL COURTS

1. STATE COURTS
   a. Trial courts of Inferior Jurisdiction—limited to civil suits involving small amounts of money and minor violations of criminal law, e.g. municipal courts, city courts, justice of the peace courts
   b. Trial Courts of General Jurisdiction (superior court, district court, circuit court)—distributed geographically through state; principal function is trial and initial determination of important civil/criminal controversies; act as appellate tribunals for appeals from judgments in inferior courts and to review actions of certain state administrative agencies

c. Specialized Trial Courts—Family, Probate
d. Intermediate, Appellate courts (Court of Appeals)—Review actions of lower courts of state
e. Court of last resort (Supreme Ct. of state)

2. FEDERAL COURTS
    a. District Courts—there are special trial courts, e.g. tax—U.S. divided into federal judicial districts; Article III, Section 1 is controlling text and sets jurisdiction bounds of courts. 3 Categories of cases seen in Federal District Courts:
        i.   Cases where U.S. is party
        ii. Cases involving a federal question and
        iii. Cases involving diversity of citizenship
        vi. Why is case in Federal Court? How did it get there?
    b. Circuit Courts, Court of Appeals—Ga. is in 11th circuit—there are 13 judicial circuits. Cases heard by panel of three judges—only way to bypass intermediate step is if trial heard by three judges on trial level
    c. U.S. Supreme Court (Article III, Section 1)—attempt to control cases that get to supreme court; WRIT OF CERTIORARI—Supreme Court will decide whether to hear case or not. Consider importance of case, split in circuit courts, decisions national in scope. Cases as a matter of right which can be heard by Court on ones where State Supreme Court has upheld validity of state law or statute against a challenge on Federal Constitutional grounds

3. Administrative Agencies—Exercise powers of adjudication
    a. Administrative Procedure Act—Federal Agencies became subject to uniform procedural standards. Enacted in 1946. Created to cope with problems of

public concern. Judicial function is to weigh merits of case vs. consistent determinations of policy

b. Reasons For Admin. Agencies Over Judicial: Need for expertise; specialization and continuity; desire for sympathetic admin.; volume of cases decided; less rigid and formal

B. STRUCTURE OF LAWSUIT

1. PROCEDURE—Mechanism through which rules of substantive law have effect

a. Identify Nature of Problem—Advise client; clients don't come in with labeled problems; evaluate case; whether it's worth pursuing; must have knowledge, research of statutes, case law, and must know facts of case

b. Pleading Stage—(representing P), File a complaint (once you have determined court which has jurisdiction and that you are certified to practice there); correct subject matter jurisdiction; can we obtain personal jurisdiction over D? Can court exercise authority over part. person/entity? Must serve complaint to individual and then file it—defendant has options:

   i. Ignore complaint, defaults. P can obtain default judgment, then an execute judgment

   ii. Attempt to attack the complaint:

      a. Motion to dismiss for failure to state cause of action (demurrer); ct. assumes facts in complaint are true and concludes that despite the facts, there is no basis for claim

   iii. Answer complaint; D may deny allegations, going towards facts, not law

   iv. Raise an affirmative defense; D agrees to facts but adds facts which create justification for change in outcome

c. Discovery Phase—Promulgation of INTERROGA-TORIES (written responses to questions posed by P) and DEPOSITIONS (oral transcript of witnesses) preserves testimony for witness that may be unavailable for trial; need permission from court to amend complaint

d. Trial—P goes first and ordinarily has burden of proof; after P rests D has options
   i. D can motion for SUMMARY JUDGMENT (during discovery phase)—viewing evidence from position most favorable to P, there is no cause of action
   ii. D can move for DIRECTED VERDICT—viewing facts most favorable to P, facts are insufficient to support P's claim
   iii. D's case presented next. After D rests, P has options:
      a. Can move for a DIRECTED VERDICT
      b. Only one possible outcome, judge should direct verdict. Rarely given
   iv. Charge to juror—Judge informs jury what law is. Parties will submit jury instructions to judge which guide jury deliberations. Either party can object to instructions on appeal. Jury then deliberates and returns verdict

e. Post-trial motions—Motion for judgment N.O.V. (judge enters verdict against jury verdict)—Motion to Set Aside Verdict and Ask for a New Trial, Motion for New Trial based on Erroneous Rulings

f. EXECUTION of judgment—Judgment becomes final unless appealed, e.g. collect monies, procedures to find out what D has and how to get it

g. If APPEALED, petition is filed, record from trial court is sent to appellate court, briefs submitted from both sides, sometimes oral arguments. Scrutinizes correctness of trial court rulings. No additional testimony is taken

h. Cases:
   i.   <u>Gumperz v. Hofmann</u>—service of process valid even though if obtained under deceit
   ii. <u>Grand Lodge v. Farnham</u>—sustained demurrer. Facts of case did not give P cause of action. Defect in plea

C. TECHNIQUE OF CASE LAW DEVELOPMENT— Understand facts of case, grounds for decision and synthesize holdings.

   1. JUDICIAL DECISIONS ON NEW QUESTIONS: CASES

      a. <u>Priestly v. Fowler</u>—Fellow servant rule, no cause of action proven against master

      b. <u>Albro v. Agawam Canal</u>—Reference made to Priestly v. Fowler; same result, no cause of action against master; fellow servant rule; could have distinguished case from precedent based on different facts and more industrial in nature but court chose not to

      c. <u>Watkins v. Clark</u>—Car is no longer considered dangerous instrument. Agency of daughter to father inapplicable because although dad owned car, daughter used it for her own purposes. In past, father would have been held liable but now P has no evidence to state cause of action. Rejected agency theory

      d. <u>King v. Smythe</u>—Car case in same year, in different jurisdiction with different results. D owning car and allowing member of his family to use for pleasure makes out prima facie case of liability. Agency rule holds.

e. <u>Watkins</u> where D was not liable. Analyzed with agency theory but did not use for judgment

f. <u>Hynes v. N.Y. Cent. R. Co.</u>—Two rules of law converge; that of a D's lack of duty to protect trespassers on land and D's duty to regulate conduct to protect travelers on adjacent public ways. Appellate court is error; D must protect those on public ways regardless of trespass

2. EFFECT OF PRECEDENT ON A SUBSEQUENT CASE—Need to learn how to distinguish cases on facts, narrowing the asserted precedent in terms of procedural issue:

a. HOLDING (ratio decidendi)—Must be followed in similar cases until overruled. Produced through "fire of controversy"

b. DICTUM—Any statement in opinion not necessary to decision of case, persuasive but not binding. Stare decisis not as strong in constitutional issues

c. CASE: <u>Cullings v. Goetz</u>—Covenant to repair does not impose lessor to liability in tort at the suit of lessee or others lawfully on land at right of lessee. Lessor only allowed on premises at lessee's request, therefore no control and can't be liable. Reference to many non-N.Y. cases which are persuasive, not binding. Prevailing doctrine of state (stare decisis) holds. Dicta to contrary not binding. Restatement of Torts reference is used as secondary source of persuasive authority.Cardozo appears to want different result but effect of stare decisis and volume of cases supports position which exists

   i. Scope of Precedent: Stare decisis—Decision in case should govern decision in all like cases, like cases based on material fact situations of cases. State holding of precedent case in sufficiently general terms so that it covers facts of your case. Key determination is policy

ii. What was policy underlying earlier decision?
Well-considered recent dictum may hold more
weight with courts than old holding

iii. Treat Like Cases Alike—Legal reasoning is a
matter of putting a case in right category.

b. GE v. Gilbert—GE provides general health insurance but excludes pregnancey. That's OK in 1976
because pregnancy is not a sex-based classification.
Singling out condition, not sub-group. Also claim
that it is elective. Suit brought on behalf of women
claiming it violated Title VII. NOTE: Congress did
not approve of this reading and later amended Title
VII to make exclusion of pregnancy an impermis-
sible discrimination

c. Fragrante v. County of Honolulu—Guy with accent
is out of luck. Accent materially interferes with job
performance; therefore, it is the effect of accent
which is objected to, not the fact he has one. In both
cases, P failed to show that non-selection was based
on any discriminatory intent or motive. Being able
to be understood by customers was a bona fide
occupational qualification for job

FORMALISM—Legal cases should be decided simply by
applying pre-existing legal rules to whatever facts are
presented without reference to any extra-legal policies
or principles. Problem with this view is that often no
logically reliable way exists to identify applicable rule,
e.g. Hynes. Makes things fit into existing rules

REALISM— Instrumentalist in outlook; takes position
that law serves social and political purposes which are
in themselves not legally distinctive. Cardozo would
be Realist. Serves goals outside legal system as equal-
ity, liberty, and justice. Allows for creation of new
rules

3. SYNTHESIS—Emphasis on learning how law has changed and why. Cases:
   a. Seixas v. Wood—No implied warranty, caveat emptor—let the buyer beware. Privity between parties
   b. Winterbottom v. Wright—Privity between parties required for liability. Coach not inherently dangerous
   c. Thomas and Wife v. Winchester—No privity between parties, however still liable due to imminent danger relating to poisonous drug. Poison is inherently dangerous. Uses Winterbottom case
   d. Loop v. Litchfield—Different from Winchester because not wheel not imminently dangerous (lasted 5 years). This is case where "inherently dangerous" comes up. No cause of action. Wheel not inherently dangerous
   e. Losee v. Clute—Dealing with property damage v. personal injury. P was out-of-loop bystander. No privity. No control over boiler maintenance and management once sold to Paper Co. No cause of action. Relies on Loop
   f. Devlin v. Smith—Watershed case; defective scaffold at 50 is imminently dangerous; refers to Winchester principle. Manufacturer of scaffold (Stevenson) liable; Devlin, employer is not. No privity between parties. Focused on defectiveness
   g. MacPherson v. Buick Motor Co.—Extension of Devlin—manufacturer had knowledge of danger of wooden wheel on car and also had knowledge that car would end up in third party's possession as sold car to retailer. A defective wheel on auto is imminently dangerous. Manufacturer responsible for finished product. More probable the danger, the

more the need for caution. Concerned with danger to society. Foreseeability. Dissent: Extends law too far. Suppose to be for inherently dangerous products

III. PROBLEM OF RETROACTIVITY

A. When judicial decision announces new rule of law or overrules old one it almost always operates retroactively. Applies to events that occurred before new or changed rule was declared. (Parties in current litigation) New rule now applied to all pending and prospective suits no matter how long before the events giving rise to suit had occurred

B. Molitor v. Kaneland Comm. Unit Dist. No. 302—School immunity; Court's duty to overrule those decisions, stare decisis and establish rule consonant with present-day concepts of right and justice. Retroactive application of decision may result in great hardships to school districts, therefore justice will best be served by holding that, except in this case, the rule established shall only apply to cases arising out of future occurrences. Overruling decision should be made PROSPECTIVE whenever injustice or hardship due to reliance to overruled decision would be averted. DOCTRINE OF PROSPECTIVE OPERA-TION—basis of doctrine is reliance upon overruled precedent. Dissent: Legislation after case provided immunity to park districts, counties, and granted limited tort immunity to schools

IV. AUTHORITATIVE STATUS OF JUDICIAL DECISIONS

A. In same court system, general rule is a court must follow decision of any court which in event of appeal can reverse decision of lower court. For decisions rendered by courts other than highest, problems arise. When decisions are from courts in different systems, there is no authoritative status although may be persuasive

B. STATUS OF STATE DECISIONS IN FEDERAL COURTS—Fed. Ct. involved in state law when U.S. is party; constitutional issue and diversity of citizenship (eliminates prejudice)

1. Erie Railroad Co. v. Tompkins—Diversity of citizenship; issue is whether Fed. Ct. is free to disregard alleged rule of state. D insisted P was trespasser under Pa. common law. District and Circuit Courts disagreed and found for P. Held that question was one of general law, not local and Fed. Ct. did not have to apply unwritten law of highest court in the state. Free to exercise independent judgment as to what common law of state is to create uniformity (Swift v. Tyson). Supreme Ct. reverses : Swift v. Tyson doctrine has revealed defects. Privilege of selecting court to try case (Fed. or State) was conferred on non-citizen of state therefore citizen did not receive equal protection of the law. Except in matters governed by Federal Constitution or Acts of Congress, the law to be applied in any case is the law of the state. This should be done whether by statute or common law courts. There is no such thing as federal general common law. Presumption of Tyson doctrine is that there is a law which transcends the states but obligatory to them within the state unless changed by state statute. Tyson overruled

2. King v. Order of United Commercial Travelers of America—Neither party found any decisions of S.C. state court on point relating to aviation exclusion clauses. District court fell back on general principles of S.C. insurance law. Court held that P's death resulted in drowning and P was entitled to recover

because state insurance law was ambiguous and any ambiguities should be resolved in favor of beneficiary. Appellate Court found same result based on District Court's holding. Never appealed to State Supreme Ct. Fed. Appellate Ct. reversed holding that there was no ambiguity in insurance law therefore, P should not recover and if it had been appealed to State Supreme court would have found the same result. Rules of Decision Act commands Federal Courts to regard as rules of decision the substantive laws of state. Issue though is what if never determined at Supreme Court level of state only by lower courts? Circuit court of appeals did right thing in that made determination as to what supreme court of S.C. would have ruled. Lower courts in state have no published records and are accorded little weight as precedents in State's own courts. Judgment for D

V. INTERPRETATION OF STATUTES—Always possibility of ambiguity; cannot paraphrase statutes—ask purpose question; do not give words a meaning that context will not support; audience of statute important in determining meaning; no statute exists in isolation; believe that legislatures are reasonable people pursuing reasonable purposes reasonably! Look to other sources as necessary

A. LEGISLATIVE PROCESS
   1. STRUCTURE, POWER, FUNCTIONS
   2. SOURCE AND DEVELOPMENT OF LEGISLATIVE PROPOSALS

B. FINDING AND STATING ISSUES OF STATUTE LAW—Identify key words of statute, what words create controversy. Designate source of key words (identify statute in issue statement). ISSUE—issue in case of statutory interpretation must be stated so as to include an

exact quotation of the precise term of statute with respect
to which the question of statutory applicability arises. No
paraphrasing permitted. What does statute say exactly with
respect to legal problem at hand?

1. PROBLEM CASE 1: Moral Turpitude? Immigration and
   Nationality Act of 1952

2. PROBLEM CASE 2: Anti-discrimination Act of 1949—
   Full & equal accommodations; advantages, privileges,
   amusement; "Except for reasons applicable alike to all
   citizens"

3. PROBLEM CASE 4: Johnson v. Southern Pacific Railroad
   —employee injured when attempting to couple freight
   engine and dining car. Does it fall within statute and
   violate it thereby making employee not assume risks of
   injury? Is locomotive engine a car? Car used in
   moving interstate traffic? Couplers coupling automati-
   cally to each other? What if trains have different brand
   couplers? Act's intent: to promote safety of employees
   and travelers upon railroads engaged in interstate
   commerce

C. RESOLVING STATUTORY ISSUES

1. Johnson v. Southern Pacific Co.—Appeal case; common law view—P assumed risks and dangers of the
   coupling which he endeavored to make and is estopped
   from recovering damages. Based on familiar rules that
   servant assumes ordinary risks and dangers of employment. Only intention expressed in law or contract that
   court can give effect to. Primary rule to interpret
   statute—ascertain the intent which legislative body that
   enacted law has expressed. Construction and interpretation have no place where terms of statute are clear
   and certain and its meaning is plain. When language of
   statute is unambiguous, and its meaning evident, it
   must be held to mean what it plainly expresses and no

room left for construction. Statute which changes common law must be strictly construed. Intention of legislature and meaning of penal statute must be found in the language actually used, interpreted according to fair and usual meaning, not in evils which it was intended to remedy. Defendant did not violate according to act. P assumes own risk of injuries. Thayer dissents to conclusion, concurs with judgment. Feels that "car" is a generic term

2. <u>Johnson v. Southern Pacific Co.</u>—Supreme Court— reverses. Circuit Court ruling is inconsistent with the intent of Congress which was to promote safety of employees and travelers upon railroads engaged in interstate commerce. Circuit court construction of statute is too narrow. Risk in coupling was evil sought to be remedied. Referred to President Messages of 4 years, Senate Reports and Debates.

D. INTERPRETATION BASED ON LEGISLATIVE IN-TENT—Other words in statute or title; speeches and committee reports; other actions and events. (intent is subjective, politics, no reason to believe Congress ever considered particular facts of this dispute). Judicial application of statute law—if doubts as to meaning or legal effect of statutory language they are to be resolved in accordance with the intention of legislature. Difficult in cases with issues unanticipated by legislature at time of enactment

1. SPECIFIC INTENT—Shows that Congress foresaw issue presented and meant to resolve it in a particular way

2. GENERAL PURPOSE—Demands that interpretive issues unforeseen specifically by legislators be resolved in a way to advance rather than retard the attainment of objectives which legislators sought to achieve by enactment

3. The technique of PURPOSE INTERPRETATION traces back to HEYDON'S CASE:
    a. Look to common law
    b. What evil did common law not address?
    c. What remedy did legislature make with statute?
    d. Construe statute to cure evil and apply legislative remedy
4. Reasons why statute may fall short of goal of perfect certainty:
    a. Words are imperfect, do not mean the same thing to all people
    b. Unforeseen situations are inevitable; make statute for specific needs in a form to give general applicability
    c. Uncertainties may be added in course of enactment; legislator likely to make changes in bill without having time to consider effect of changes on bill as a whole. Amendments may add confused or inconsistent provisions
        i. Holy Trinity Church v. United States—Uncertainty not created by words but factual circumstances; statute broad but clear. Specific and general purpose. Rule that a thing may be within letter of statute and yet not within the statute, because not within spirit or intention of its makers. Considered whole legislation, circumstances surrounding enactment. The reason of law in such cases should prevail over its words. Court looked at title, evil it was designed to remedy, petitions and testimony presented to Congress and Report of Senate Committee to determine legislative intent
        ii. The People Ex Rel. Fyfe v. Barnett—Specific Intent—Eliminated P's name from jury list; D said P did not possess necessary legal qualifica-

tions for jury duty because she was a woman. Women given limited right of suffrage in Illinois in 1913 but general statute relating to jurors was enacted as amended in 1899. Intention of legislature at the time of enactment should be ascertained. Words of statute must be taken in sense in which understood at time of enactment. At the time of passage, providing for appointment of a jury commission and making jury lists, the words "voters" and "electors" were not ambiguous. The legislature at that time defined those terms by the constitution and laws of State which did not include women, as Suffrage Act and 19th amendment had not yet been enacted. The word electors in statute meant male persons only to the legislators who enacted it. P not entitled to sit on jury. Reversed

iii. <u>Commonwealth v. Maxwell</u>—General Purpose—D tried to quash indictment for murder because woman sat on grand jury. Jury selection statute enacted in 1867 and 19th amendment allowing women the right to be electors did not occur until later. Act refers to "qualified electors." Jury commissioners are required to select "from the whole qualified electors of the respective county." 19th amendment has placed women in this category as the term "elector" is a generic term (not specific). Act's intent is to take in new classes of electors as they come to the voting privilege from time to time. Statutes framed in general terms apply to new cases that arise, and to new subjects that are created which come within their general scope and policy. Case reversed because woman is allowed to sit on jury so murder indictment holds

E. PLAIN MEANING RULE—Use plain meaning unless absurd results; words in isolation can't always be clear; words are only meaningful in context. Two types of context : legislative (solution to public problem), and case (whether dispute is one which statute addresses). Where the act is clear upon its face and is fairly susceptible to one construction, that construction must be used. Where words conflict with each other or are inconsistent, construction becomes necessary and a departure from the obvious meaning of words is justifiable. But, if the plain meaning of a provision is to be disregarded because we believe the framers of that act could not intend what they say, it must be one in which absurdity and injustice of applying the provision to the case would be so monstrous that all mankind would without hesitation unite in rejecting the application

1. Caminetti v. United States—Broad interpretation; Court took plain language to determine judgment. Conviction and sentence for violation of White Slave Traffic Act of 1910; P's argument: Congress intended to reach only commercialized vice or the traffic of women for gain. P's acts not within the meaning of statute when properly construed in light of its history and the purposes intended by its enactment. Court rationale: If language of statute is plain, court's sole function is to enforce it. No ambiguity in this Act. Key words are "any other immoral purpose." P's actions were for immoral purpose. While title of Act cannot overcome plain meaning and unambiguous words used, the title here refers to immoral purposes. When words are free from doubt they must be taken as the final expression of legislative intent. Does not lead to absurd result. Affirmed. McKenna's dissent: If words ambiguous we are not exempt from putting ourselves in place of legislators. Must take title and all

parts of statute into consideration to ascertain meaning. Title White Slave Act connotes commercialized vices and court has interpreted immoral purposes in too broad a manner. Legislative records are also persuasive

2. <u>Chung Fook v. White</u>—Wife of a native-born U.S. citizen is detained at immigration station because she is alien and has contagious disease. Immigration Act of 1917 allows wife of naturalized citizen to be admitted to U.S. as citizen and immediately seek treatment of disease. Plain words of statute do not allow court to interpolate this to extend to native-born citizen's wives. Remedy lies with Congress to make this change which discriminates against native-born citizens, not with the courts. Plain meaning applies.

F. DEVELOPMENT OF CURRENT DOCTRINE (assume legislature is supreme, role of court is to interpret as delegate of legislature, judges not charged with rewriting law)

1. Read statute first, what is it trying to exclude and include —What is it silent on?

2. Read statute with eye to facts of case

3. Read statute looking for intent

4. Read data surrounding statute

5. Develop hypothesis

6. Test hypothesis against wider circles of context

7. Determine if have legislative intent or purpose

8. Public policy concerns.

9. What are administration's general considerations? Have codes been in effect for long periods of time? Look to prior decisions of agency. Remember that Congress has had opportunities to change regs.

10. <u>United States v. American Trucking Ass'ns</u>—ICC to establish reasonable requirements regarding qualifica-

tions and maximum hours of service of employees of motor carriers. Which employees can be regulated by policies, drivers or all employees including clerical? Conflict in scope of word "employees." Plain meaning answer would have been yes. Watershed Case regarding looking outside of statute's language. Start with plain meaning then intrinsic aids then extrinsic aids then other law on the subject, then post-enactment history (after law was enacted, what was the result?) and if all else fails, look to policy. May arrive at specific intent but more likely to arrive at general purpose of statute

G. WEIGHT OF PRIOR INTERPRETATIONS

    1. <u>Girouard v. United States</u>—Canadian seeking citizenship can serve America as citizen without bearing arms. Prior decisions held this not to be the case but Court now recognizes that religious belief is basic in a society of free men. This decision may prompt Congress to act but it is a judge-made rule that overrules prior decisions. Court refuses to interpret Congress' silence on this issue to mean they approve of prior decisions. This decision updates social policy

    2. <u>Cleveland v. United States</u>—Mormons took wives over state lines. Caminetti controls—silence by Congress is not consent however if court is not willing to overrule Caminetti then it is still affirmative law

H. MAXIMS, CANONS—Canons do not give answer, they only help justify an answer which you reach by other means. Maxim—analytical starting point

VI. COORDINATION OF JUDGE-MADE AND STATUTE LAW—Stare decisis—only apply if substantial reliance, apply if it would encourage efficient judicial administration (equal parties treated equally) One-shot theory—first statutory

interpretation should be followed always. Aspect of coordination is court's role in expounding statutes. Court acts as co-legislature in extending or not extending statutes or constitutional limitations by looking at policy. If statute is unclear then the courts may look to see purpose of statute by assisting Congress to define law. No mandatory requirement to reason policy where no statute exists. No federal common law but reality of this is arguable when statute changing common law comes into effect since federal courts could say it has wide application. Where statute is remedial it gets broad interpretation. ROSCOE POUND—

A. Cannon v. University of Chicago—Cites Cort v. Ash as precedent. Woman thought she was excluded from medical school due to sex.

   1. Was statute enacted for special class of which P is member? (Whether P fall within category of sex discrimination by recipients of federal funds)

   2. Does legislative history of statute indicate that Congress intended to create such a remedy? Look at statute in its entirety and look at similar statutes enacted at about the same time. If language is the same, look to the construction that has been given and Congress' reaction to that construction.

   3. Would implication of private remedy frustrate the underlying purpose of the legislative scheme?

   4. Is implication of federal remedy inappropriate because the subject matter involves an area basically of concern to the state? Powell dissented because he wanted more rigid test. These four factors too elastic for him

B. Public Citizen v. U.S. Department of Justice—ABA Committee on Federal Judiciary gave recommendations to President on Supreme Court nominees. Does the Federal Advisory Committee Act apply to the ABA? At plain meaning, rule that ABA falls under the statute but this is not necessarily a reasonable interpretation. Absurdity is not the test here. Key work is "utilized." As in American Trucking, scope of the key word's definition would be inconsistent with Congress' true purpose in writing the statute. ABA committee is used in a different way than committees that fall under government control. The GSA lacked the expertise to define "utilized"

C. Chevron U.S.A. Inc. v. Natural Resources Defense Council, Incl. Et Al.—EPA says emissions requirements apply to the total of plants in a given geographical region (bubble). Court looked at EPA as having expertise ("Stationary source"). If Congress' intent is not discernible and the EPA's regulations are "reasonable" then the court is bound within the limitations of outrageousness so the EPA limits the court's discretion

D. Touche Ross—Whether customers of securities. Relies more on second prong of Cort where all four factors were not all entitled to equal weight and that congressional intent (here judged negative) was determinative

E. United States v. Thompson Center Arms Co.—Is it a firearm when you have to put it together yourself? Parallel to Johnson because the statute is a punitive tax statute that must be strictly construed (based on the maxim).

F. Thompson v. Thompson—Parent Kidnapping prevention Act of 1980. Was Congress inviting public to maintain private causes of action? Statute is silent on intent. So, does the third Cort factor outweigh the others so that allowing private cause of action complies with the intent of Congress? Held—no private cause of action because none of factors inferred one. Just because the legislative history does not create a cause when the other three Cort factors don't point that way

G. Immigration and Naturalization Service v. Chadha—
Coordination of separation of powers. Congress usurped
the executive branch by giving decision power to Attorney
General but maintained a veto power. Both houses of
Congress must partake in veto but did not. Court says its a
violation of separation of powers

E. Planned Parenthood v. Casey —workability; reliance;
right to personal integrity; court credibility; subsequent
decisions—has evolution of legal principles undercut
foundation of Roe v. Wade? Some cases unpermissibly
extended Roe so overruled peripheral developments of it
but kept its cornerstone holding. Qualitative determination on how binding stare decisis should be is made on a
case-by-case basis. Gave some guidance to legislative
bodies. Court also chunked "trimester" test in favor of
viability. Focused on undue burden and the state's interest. DUE PROCESS CLAUSE as it relates to abortion
rights. Three primary inquiries:

1. Whether rule of law court is considering applying was
correctly decided. Roe v. Wade does not lead to
absurd results so should not overrule it

2. Has precedent been relied on extensively so that overruling would be harmful?

3. Have factual and/or doctrinal underpinnings eroded?

CIVIL PROCEDURE II

I. DESCRIBING AND DEFINING THE DISPUTE

A. COMMON LAW PLEADING

1. Got into royal court by writ (similar to summons). Significance—there were different writs for different wrongs claimed, e.g. trespass.

2. Great detail of requirements relating to different forms of action. Needed to establish all details and requirements—very rigid. Different procedures for different writs.

3. Were not many different forms of writs. Writ system developed fictions to cover other types of actions— caused trickery.

4. No joinder or pleading in the alternative existed. If chose wrong writ, can't go back and plead alternatively. Pleading system was inordinately important because there were no big trials.

5. Goals of pleading were to identify and isolate particular fact or legal issue to be disputed in case. Better pleader usually won case—not because they had better merits.

6. Showed blueprint of trial, all facts, notice and screening. Pleading with particularity.

7. Equity courts grew due to writ system rigidity. Law courts did not give injunctions or specific performance.

B. AMERICAN REFORMS—FIELD CODE (started in NY) —less formality

1. Abolished separate courts of law and equity

2. Abolished separate forms of action; same procedures for all forms

3. All you had to do was set forth facts sufficient to constitute cause of action; no legal fictions necessary.

4. Have complaint, answer and reply—not trying to distill down to one issue of fact or law.

5. Retain ability to obtain demurrer

6. <u>Gillispie v. Goodyear Service Stores</u>—b & c interpreted harshly in case. Holding: Must state facts sufficient to constitute a cause of action. Can't plead conclusions.

7. PURPOSE FOR PLEADING
   a. Notice of nature of claim to D
   b. Identify issues in dispute to govern court in conduct of trial
   c. Narrows issues—apprise parties of factual allegations
   d. Screen out baseless claims—the more specificity, the more claims could be screened out

C. MODERN PLEADING: THE PLAINTIFF'S CLAIM—RULE 8

1. Reformed Field Code by deleting word "fact" & by omitting cause of action. Just plead facts that support claim. Primary function is notice to D. If specific enough to put D on notice, but miss element, may still withstand motion to dismiss under Rule 8. Rule 8 is weak on preventing baseless claims because of vagueness of requirements. Delays functions to other devices, e.g. discovery to narrow issues, provide blueprint for trial and screen out baseless claims.

2. Federal Rule takes on less ambitious role to pleadings because sometimes Ps don't know how, e.g. negligence, occurred.

3. Movement back the other way because has become too easy to sue D. Discovery process expensive. Want to eliminate cases in early stage of pleading. Tension between P & D concerns.

4. PROBLEM OF SPECIFICITY—P not required to plead legal theory—must plead basic facts. Rule 8(a)—fair notice of claim; Shall contain:
   a. Short and plain statement of grounds upon which court's jurisdiction depends;
   b. Short and plain statement that shows P entitled to relief and;
   c. Demand for judgment for relief pleader seeks.
   d. Rule 9—requires specific pleading in cases of fraud and mistake because just by filing these suits, can damage D's reputation making them vulnerable to settlement.
   e. <u>United States v. Board of Harbor Commissioners</u>—Question is does D have enough information to prepare response, not does D have enough information to defend!
      i. Rule 12(e)—Motion for more definite statement.
      ii. Rule 11—Motion not grounded in fact or law.
5. CONSISTENCY AND HONESTY IN PLEADING
   a. <u>McCormick v. Kopmann</u>—P has right to go to trial on conflicting counts enumerated in complaint to ease judicial administration. Lack of certainty enables P to plead contradicting counts. Had to do it this way because at C/L there was no joinder. Rule 8(a)—allows pleading in the alternative. OK so long as pleader has no knowledge of true facts. Rule 8(e)(2)
   b. <u>Albright v. Upjohn Co.</u>—Rule 11 case. Difference between old and new Rule 11—emphasis on certification prior to new rule was whether it was filed in bad faith for improper purposes vs. new rule—Reasonable inquiry prior to file to determine and firm belief that case is
      i. well grounded in fact and
      ii. well grounded in law.

c. Holding: P under Rule 11 must establish affirmative evidence to support claim at time complaint is made. No reasonable likelihood that P would ever obtain evidence needed therefore no factual basis for case against D.

d. Rule 11 (old) signing lawyer was liable but under new rule, law firm is also liable.

    i. Old rule—sanctions mandatory with discretion in choice of sanction.

    ii. New rule—court has discretion to impose sanction. Sanction issue softening so as not to discourage Ps from certain claims, e.g. <u>Brown v. Board of Education.</u> New rule is a deterrence model—does not necessarily like monetary sanctions, may use censure. Monetary sanctions of choice are to pay court, not to compensate other side.

e. Safe Harbor Rule—can withdraw pleading to avoid sanctions.

6. SCRUTINIZING THE LEGAL SUFFICIENCY OF PLAINTIFF'S CLAIM

    a. <u>Mitchell v. Archibald & Kendall, Inc.</u>

7. HEIGHTENED REQUIREMENTS FOR SPECIFICITY

    a. <u>Ross v. A.H. Robins Company</u>—Rule 9 Case. Holding: Rule 9(b) requires circumstances constituting fraud be stated with particularity and with specificity so that D has knowledge of facts indicating that their actions led to P's conclusions relating to fraud and misconduct. Particularity is needed because allegations are so harmful to reputation of D & this increased level will reduce weaker claims. Rule 9—must plead special damages (damages not originally arising out of situation) specifically. General damages—damages that flow from wrong, e.g. wages.

b. <u>Albany Welfare Rights Org. Day Care Center, Inc. v. Schreck</u>—In some cases, courts have held non-Rule 9 cases to Rule 9 standards because it's so easy to allege certain causes of action, e.g. retaliation, and court needs to protect D.

c. <u>Leatherman v. Tarrant City</u>—Holding: Federal Court may not apply heightened pleading standard, more stringent than usual requirements, in civil rights cases alleging municipal liability under Section 1983.

d. RULE 7—Pleadings allowed; forms of motions—p.26.

e. RULE 10—Form of pleadings; Tells form of pleading, e.g #'d paragraphs—p. 35.

D. DEFENDANT'S RESPONSE AND DISMISSALS

1. PRE-ANSWER MOTIONS UNDER RULE 12—must be filed within 20 days of summons. If motion denied, have 10 days after motion to file answer. (Ga. have 30 days—whether file motion or not to answer). Main vehicle for filing motion—Rule 12 (Pre-trial)—D's options to dismiss case early.

a. 12(b) contains seven motions:
   i. Lack of subject matter jurisdiction
   ii. Lack of personal jurisdiction
   iii. Improper venue
   iv. Insufficiency of process
   v. Insufficiency of service of process
   vi. Failure to state claim upon which relief can be granted; modern day demurrer
   vii. Failure to join party under Rule 19

b. If D prevails, P's complaint will be dismissed without prejudice except 12(b)(6)

c. 12(c)—not pre-trial motion; like 12(b)(6) except can make this after the answer or at closing of pleadings.

Considers D's pleadings. Motion to dismiss on pleadings.

d. 12(e)—Motion for more definite statement—used when D can't answer due to lack of intelligibility.

e. 12(g)—need to consolidate motions; make them all at the same time

f. 12(h)—provides that certain defenses will be waived if not made in certain period of time. Subject matter jurisdiction is never waived. Disfavored defenses must be made on first response or else they're waived, e.g. personal jurisdiction, venue, and service of process.

g. Two different kinds of 12(b)(vi) challenges:
   i. Quantitative—did not specifically state facts even though had ground for relief; court will be more likely to dismiss without prejudice or grant request to amend; and
   ii. Qualitative—plead factual specificity, but law does not give relief here.

2. FAILURE TO ANSWER—DEFAULT
   a. <u>Shepard Claims Service, Inc. v. William Darrah & Associates</u>—Holding: where defaulting party satisfies first 2 requirements for relief (meritorious defense and no prejudice to P) and moves promptly to set aside default before it is entered, court should grant motion if party offers credible explanation for delay and does not exhibit disregard for judicial proceedings. D/C has discretion to assess sanction on attorney.

3. THE ANSWER—to be filed within 20 days of summons. Respond to merits. D's answer looked at the same way as P's complaint—notice.
   a. Rule 8(b)—requirements for answer; short, concise, and plain terms—either admit, deny, or respond that

there is insufficient information to answer. D can plead in the alternative and plead every possible defense.

 i. Admitting or denying the averments—can admit or deny allegations

 ii. Types of Denials:

  a. General—denies each and every allegation in P's complaint. Risky because if it comes out that you did know one averment was true then you will be deemed as admitting all averments.

  b. Specific—deny statement in specific paragraph

  c. Qualified—admit parts but not all.

 iii. Denial of knowledge has the effect of a denial.

b. Rule 8(c)—defense must be specifically pled; certain types; 19 defenses. Can list an affirmative defense that is not listed in Rule 8. D must plead affirmative defenses.

c. Four factors to determine who has to plead defense (not listed in 8(c)):

 i. Who has burden of proof at trial—that person should raise defense in pleading

 ii. Fairness

 iii. Public Policy

 iv Probability that person had the evidence needed.

d. <u>David v. Crompton & Knowles Corp.</u>—Holding: Of a matter alleged in answer that was of record and within the control and knowledge of D, an answer that D was without knowledge or information sufficient to form a belief did not constitute a denial under Rule 8(b) and is therefore considered as being admittedly true. Failure to deny—admit. Failure to deny effectively or properly—admit.

e. Affirmative Defenses—Up to D to allege defenses that would disprove P's claim. P does not need to show affirmative defenses in complaint.

f. <u>Gomez v. Toledo</u>—Holding: Only two required allegations to P's cause of action must be made:
    i. Person has deprived him of federal right and
    ii. that person acted under color of law. Not necessary for P to allege qualified immunity which is an affirmative defense of D. P does not have to show bad faith to defense in pleading.

g. Rule 8 (c) refers to affirmative defenses which must be pled by D. Waived if D does not raise it in answer unless amended. List of defenses under rule are not exhaustive.

E. AMENDMENTS AND ATTENDANT PROBLEMS
 1. PERMISSION TO AMEND
    a. <u>David v. Crompton & Knowles Corp.</u>—Holding: Where amendment has been unduly delayed or would result in prejudice to other party, court will deny motion to amend. Here D's amendment from admit to denial after the statue of limitations has run would severely prejudice P. D had reasonable duty of inquiry; can't use lack of information when you have information in your control and could have just looked it up. Court viewed lack of knowledge and information as an admission.

 2. RELATION BACK OF AMENDMENTS—when s/o/l has run and P wants to amend and have amendment given same date as original.
    a. Types of Relation Back Amendments:
       i. Adds New Legal Theory—OK when claim or defense arose out of same transaction or occurrence as original claim or defense.

    ii. Add New Party—must have:
- a. arisen out of same transaction, and
- b. within the period required by Rule 4(m)—p. 226—for service of process
- c. party that brought in by amendment receives such notice that they won't be prejudiced by defending on merits, and
- d. knew or should have known that "but for" a mistake concerning identity of proper party, the action would have been brought against them originally.

b. <u>Swartz v. Gold Dust Casino, Inc.</u>—Holding: where claim asserted in amended pleading arose from same circumstance as original, D received notice of action within limitation period and D should have known that but for a mistake concerning identity of proper party that action would have been brought against him, P's motion to amend to add D will be granted.

c. RULE 15—Amendment
- i. 15(a)—Pre-trial amendments. If the pleading you seek to amend requires an answer, then you can amend anytime before answer is filed (no prejudice). If no response is required, can answer as a matter of right within 20 days of service—can amend as matter of right within that period. After 20 days, court can grant permission to amend (very liberal). Usually amendment is only denied if there is prejudice to other party.
- ii. 15(b)—amend during trial. Can amend during trial with permission. Court is very liberal in granting except where there is prejudice to other party. Pleadings are deemed to be amended to conform to proof.

iii. Amended—15(c)—p. 230-—P may add claim if can show that new claim relates back to original claim, conduct, occurrence or transaction. some kind of notice which would establish lack of prejudice to new party. But for mistake it would have been you.

iv. 15(c)(1)—Relation back can occur if law that provides the s/o/l expressly provides for relation back.

v. 15(c)(2)—Can add new legal theory when claim or defense arose out of same transaction or occurrence as original claim or defense. (common evidence).

II. JOINDER OF PARTIES AND CLAIMS

A. PROPER PARTIES TO A SUIT—First make sure P is proper P to sue on claim.

1. REAL PARTY IN INTEREST

   a. <u>Virginia Electric & Power Company v. Westinghouse Electric Corporation</u>—partial subrogation—either party can sue as long as both are parties in interest. Holding: A partial subrogee can be joined under Rule 19:

      i. if feasible (not feasible because it would destroy diversity jurisdiction or improper venue). Under Rule 19

      ii. if partial subrogee is not indispensable so as to prevent suit from going forward then can go forward without them. If indispensable, case is dismissed.

2. FICTITIOUS NAMES—can't sue under fictitious name unless claim arises out of activities of a highly sensitive and highly personal nature or bona-fide ignorance as to name of D. Otherwise, public has right to know what is going on at courthouse.

a. <u>Southern Methodist University Association of Women Law Students v. Wynne and Jaffe</u>—Holding: No express congressional grant of right to proceed anonymously exists nor a compelling need to protect the privacy in this matter, so Ps may not sue under fictitious names.

b. RULE 17—(Real Party in Interest) originally intended to expand class of those who may sue to include persons having equitable or beneficial interest. To reduce frivolous claim, P must have cause of action for which relief can be granted (12-b-6).

c. We need Rule 17 for historical reasons— if assigned K right to someone else, that person would stand in the original K party's shoes, however, law courts reluctant to recognize rights of assignees to K (equity did). How did innocent party (assignee) get into law court? Use litigation—assignor would sue on behalf of assignee. Rule 17 came up to eliminate this—gets rid of use litigation. Now, if Real Party In Interest, assignee, has legitimate claim they can sue under Rule 17.

d. Rule 17 is a procedural rule not substantive. It does not define the real party in interest. Look to substantive law to determine who has right to sue.

e. Requires P to have a real pecuniary interest.

f. 17(a)— Real parties in interest—every action should be pursued. Determined by looking at substantive law—who has standing to bring action. Look at who will ultimately benefit from judgment. Rule—Action must be brought by person who possesses right to enforce claim and who has significant interest in litigation—determined by substantive law of state.

B. JOINDER OF CLAIMS— @ C/L, could only bring one claim against D. If you had two related claims against D, each would have been filed as a seporate writ with the court, if different writs, so had to be heard separately. If you had two claims under one writ, e.g. two unrelated assaults, you could sue on them together.

1. COUNTERCLAIMS—offensive claim of relief between opposing parties. Cross-claim—an offensive claim between co-parties.

   a. <u>Wigglesworth v. Teamsters Local Union No. 592</u>— Holding: Counter-claims are permissive where there is no connection between the events giving rise to them and the transaction or occurrence on which P's claim is based. A claim without independent jurisdictional support must be dismissed.

2. VOLUNTARY DISMISSAL

   a. <u>D.C. Electronics, Inc. v. Nartron Corp.</u>—Rule 41(a)(1)(i)—permits dismissal of action by unilateral filing of notice of dismissal to court and provides for judicial discretion in dismissal.

3. RULE 13—(a)—Compulsory counter-claim—test is that suit must arise out of same transaction or occurrence as opposing party's claim. Exception: Does not require presence of compulsory 3rd party if court can't acquire jurisdiction. Do not need to file claim if at time of action the claim is subject to another action or opposing party brought suit upon claim by attachment. If fail to file compulsory claim at onset, you forfeit chance to file later unless couldn't bring in because of lack of jurisdiction.

   a. 13(b)—Permissive counter-claims—Pleading may state as counter-claim any claim against opposing party not arising out of the same transaction or occurrance as opposing party's claim. Do not waive your right to bring up later if don't file initially. Need independent jurisdiction.

b. 13(g)—Cross-claim—D can file cross-claim when claim arises out of same transaction or occurrence as original action or counterclaim, however don't have to assert if you don't want to.

c. 13(h)—D can use Rule 19 and 20 to bring in any other parties when necessary or permissive to counter or cross-claim.

    i. Factors to look at to see if counter -claim is compulsory are time, evidence, and events. Must determine degree of overlap to see if there is judicial economy and efficiency.

    ii. Kaminshine's opinion is that court will err in favor of compulsory counter-claim at jurisdiction phase but will err in favor of permissive at bar stage.

4. RULE 18—Joinder of Claims and Remedies—very broad rule. Allows P to bring in multiple claims against D if related or unrelated (so long as you have no jurisdiction problems). Cross references Rule 42, which tells judge that multiple claims brought against one D can be severed based on judicial discretion.

a. If any claims lack diversity or Federal Question in F/C, then no jurisdiction unless relatedness is shown with supplemental jurisdiction.

b. Practical Restrictions to Rule 18—

    i. In F/C, jurisdiction will limit P's ability to bring in unrelated claims under Rule 18, due to supplemental jurisdiction requirements;

    ii. If in F/C for diversity, a claim that is less than $50,000 will limit ability to bring claim into court.

    iii. Allows you to bring in everything but does not obligate you to do so however, doctrine of res judicata may require you to do so (defines claim as all aspects of dispute that are part of same transaction—Joinder Rules 19 & 20)—can't piecemeal dispute.

C. PERMISSIVE JOINDER OF PARTIES—Rule 20—@ C/L, generally 2 Ps could not join claims against D unless they had legally joint claims and then they had to sue together.

1. <u>Kedra v. City of Philadelphia</u>—Holding: Claims against Ds arise out of same transaction, occurrence or series of transactions or occurrences for purposes of Rule 20(a), therefore joinder of Ds in this case is proper. Court retains flexibility to sever portions of case or take other remedial actions, if necessary, once prejudice issue is more clearly formed.

2. <u>Cohen v. District of Columbia National Bank</u>

3. RULE 20 (A)—Permissive Joinder—P can join multiple Ds when claims arise out of same transaction, occurrence, or series of transactions or occurrence or if any question of law and fact common to all persons will arise in the action. Policy: Judicial economy due to duplication of evidence; consistency; avoid judicial embarrassment due to different results in separate cases.

   a. Test eliminates most of the liberality of Rule 18.

   b. Once D is in court properly under Rule 20, can then bring unrelated claims against him.

   c. Look at overlapping evidence.

4. RULE 21—Misjoinder and Non-Joinder of Parties—court may drop or sever parties that shouldn't have been brought.

D. COMPULSORY JOINDER OF PARTIES—Misjoinder is not grounds for dismissal of action. When parties must be joined in law suit. Rule 19.

1. <u>Pulitzer-Polster v. Pulitzer</u>

2. RULE 19—COMPULSORY JOINDER—D motions to dismiss for failure to join a necessary party 12 (b)(7)—triggers Rule 19 (a).

a. 19 (A)—Person is to be joined, if in his absence, complete relief can't be accorded among those already parties to suit or person claims an interest relating to subject of action and is so situated that the disposition of the action in person's absence may:
   i.   as a practical matter, impair or impede person's ability to protect that interest or
   ii. leave any persons already parties subject to substantial risk of incurring multiple or inconsisitant obligations by reason of the claimed interest. Examines the relationship between absentee and current parties to suit with a test. If joinder is feasible, party must be brought in. Three circumstances defining requisite relationship needed for compulsory joinder:
      a. (a)(i)—complete relief can't be accorded to parties currently in suit in absence of some other person
      b. *(a)(2)(i)—absentee's interest could be prejudiced as a practical matter.
      c. *(a)(2)(ii)—risks to existing party if absentee isn't brought in.
   iii. Read in disjunctive.
   iv. *Main factors in test. If joinder is not feasible, e.g. destroys diversity, venue improper, then look to 19(b) factors.

b. 19 (b)—Can proceed without real party in interest so long as P and/or D are not prejudice. Options are to dismiss or proceed without party. Factors:
   i.   P's interest in Federal forum—Is there an alternative forum where P could get relief without joinder problem?

    ii. D's interest in avoiding multiple litigation;

   iii. Absentees' interest in avoiding prejudice from proceeding;

   iv Court's interest in complete, consistent, and efficient settlement of controversies.

E. IMPLEADER (THIRD PARTY COMPLAINTS)—Rule 14—Procedural device to allow D to resolve indemnification, contribution questions in first suit. Must satisfy personal jurisdiction, due process, etc. Venue—no independent requirement. Can implead joint tortfeasors due to right of contribution. Court need not implead when it is reasonably clear that D will defeat P. Can implead when there is an implied warranty between D and 3PD. If 3PP brings in non-diverse 3PD—this does not destroy diversity, even if P and 3PD are non-diverse because P did not bring in 3rd party.

1. Must look to substantive law of state. If state does not recognize joint and several tortfeasors as being able to seek contribution, then D would not be able to bring in a joint tortfeasor through impleader.

2. Leaseway Warehouses, Inc. v. Carlton—liability damage is derivative of breach of implied warranty suit.

3. RULE 14—D (3rd party P) may bring in 3rd party who is or may be liable to D for all or part of P's claim against D; 3rd Party D may assert against P all defenses 3PP has to P's claim. Kinds of claims that D can bring in are very narrow—derivative suits, e.g. contribution, indemnity, vicarious liability, etc.,—e.g., D can bring in insurance co. because could be found liable in first suit and then insurance co. in second suit can prove that D was not liable and then D would be out of luck!

F. INTERPLEADER—Device where disinterested stakeholder goes into court and all interested parties must come in and compete for stake. Protects stakeholder from multiple liability.

1. Historically, requirements were demanding. Competing claimants' claims had to be for same amount and each claim had to derive from same source, e.g. competing heirs. C/L stakeholder had to be disinterested. Now can be interested party.

2. Essential substantive requirement today—stakeholder must show competing claimants exist to the fund.

3. Why is there a Federal Statutory remedy when there is no substantive Federal issue?

   a. Insurance and banking industries—claimants will typically be from different states.

   b. Interpleader developed prior to Int'l Shoe so in in-personam claim couldn't get personal jurisdiction over people from different states because no minimum contacts standard or long-arm statutes.

4. Federal Interpleader—18 U.S.C. 1335 makes it easy for stakeholders to gain jurisdiction over claimants:

   a. NW service of process out of F/C. Rule 22 follows Rule 4 service requirements.

   b. Eased venue rules. Proper venue where any claimant resides

   c. Diversity satisfied if there is minimal diversity between any two claimants. Only care about diversity of claimants. Rule 22 requires complete diversity.

   d. Any claim of $500 or more

   e. Related statute giving F/C injunction power over competing claimants and issues taking place in other litigation. 28 U.S.C. 1335

5. Why need federal rule and statute? Probably don't. All Rule 22 does is recognize F/C ability to grant interpleader. Substantive rules are the same. Can't use Rule 22 to do NW service of process.

6. Statutory interpleader more attractive due to procedural advantages.

7. Interpleader can't be used as device to force (funnel) all claims into one court to determine underlying liability.

8. <u>State Farm Fire & Casualty Co. v. Tashire</u>

9. RULE 22 & 28 U.S.C. 1335

G. INTERVENTION—Rule 24(a)—similar to Rule 19 in that may prejudice absent party if not let in and needs to be a certain interest that absent party can identify. Differences between rules: 19 requires that existing parties ask for other party to be joined whereas Rule 24 the absent party asks to be joined.

1. Intervention by right—either statute specifically allows it or 3 factors must be met:

   a. Absent party has direct, substantial, legally protected interest in the subject matter of the suit

   b. If not joined, this person's interest will be impaired as a practical matter

   c. Absent party must show their interest is not adequately represented by party not already in suit.

2. Rule 20 and 24(b) are both permissive joinders but in Rule 20, P has discretion and in Rule 24(b)—D has discretion.

   a. <u>Natural Resources Defense Council, Inc. v. United States Nuclear Regulatory Commission</u>

3. DEFINITION OF "INTEREST" IN RULE 24(a)(2)— require more than general public interest.

   a. <u>New Orleans Public Service, Inc. v. United Gas Pipe Line Company</u>

4. RULE 24 (a)—Anyone shall have right to intervene in an action

   a. when a statute of US confers an unconditional right to intervene; or

b. applicant claims an interest relating to property or transaction which is subject of action and applicant is so situated that the disposition of action may as a practical matter impair or impede the applicant's ability to protect that interest, unless the applicant's interest is adequately represented by existing parties.

H. **PERMISSIVE INTERVENTION**—24(b)—Permissive intervention—anyone may be permitted to intervene in an action

1. when US statute confers conditional right to intervene; or

2. when an applicant's claim or defense and the main action have a question of law or fact in common. In exercising its discretion, the court shall consider whether the intervention will unduly delay or prejudice the adjudication of rights of original parties.

3. 18 U.S.C. 1367—limits P's ability to intervene. If P is intervening as matter of right and this P is destroying diversity jurisdiction, then this P will not be allowed to raise supplemental jurisdiction. If D is intervening, he will be allowed to raise supplemental jurisdiction. An intervening P must have independent subject matter jurisdiction.

III. **DISCOVERY**—process for compelling disclosure through court-enforced rules. Seek witnesses, names, doctor testimony, etc. Serves to reduce surprises, narrow issues, screen out meritless claims, prepare for trial, promote settlement.

A. **PROMISE AND REALITY OF BROAD DISCOVERY**—Criticism about discovery is that it takes an excessive amount of time, expensive, cumulative, and burdensome, contains evasive answers, forces other side to go to court to compel information. However, many substantive law cases would not have been possible without discovery, e.g. product liability, civil rts., etc.

B. RULE 26 & AMENDMENTS!!!

1. 26(a)—Initial Disclosures—within ten days after initial meeting of parties. Tension between notice pleading and what you need to know yet.

2. 26(b)—added in 1980; 2nd P.—places limitations by court on duplicative discovery, time and unduly burdensome or expensive. (iii)—Not used often—unduly burdensome or expensive. Arms a court, however, to be able to limit discovery if they want to. Prior to this, no guidelines to allow court to get involved.

3. 26(c)—Protective Orders—procedural device for seeking protection. File a motion to court for a protective order and can put in cause of action for 2nd P. of 26(b).

   a. Up until recently, discovery was a request and one never had the obligation to send anything not asked for. Now—certain mandatory disclosures must be made without regard to discovery.

   b. Rules state that you must disclose all witnesses and damages sought without being asked for it.

   c. Other modern rules mandate that early in process, parties must have a meeting, focusing on issues, talk settlement, provide mandatory disclosure information (or within 10 days from meeting).

4. 26(f)—Meeting of parties. Revised rule makes this mandatory. As soon as practicable, and if act in bad faith there can be sanctions. Basically need to develop plan of discovery to submit to court in scheduling conference.

C. DISCOVERY DEVICES—3 Main types: Request for Production of documents (only between parties); written interrogatories (between parties); Oral depositions (not limited to parties—can be used for any witness).

1. RULE 34: DOCUMENT INSPECTION—Request for Production of Documents or Inspection of Property. Initiated by document and other side is asked to produce enumerated documents.

   a. Key Problem: How do you describe what you want clearly enough so other side can't weasel out of answering it? State with particularity. However, don't always know, that's why you're requesting information!

   b. Do not have to request document by name, but by category.

   c. Other party can object because unduly burdensome, outside scope, asking for confidential information, vague, etc.

2. RULE 33: INTERROGATORIES—Should use this device first. May learn more so can better request documents. Limited to parties. Requester serves on other side, written questions which will be returned within 30 days by other side. Lawyer writes and answers questions. Basic information is good to obtain by this method.

   a. Long been abused because don't trust other side and ask long questions to cover every loophole possible. This is a frequent source of discovery abuse and disputes.

   b. Generally have duty to make reasonable inquiry to produce information the other side wants.

   c. Have option to form of response when information is contained in document itself. If it would be no more burdensome for requesting party to view documents, can respond that they can come in and look.

d. Contention Interrogatories are permitted but not about eyewitnesses. Do not have to answer pure legal questions, e.g. what cases support your position?

e. Can use answers to interrogatories as evidence-in-chief at trial if made by party to suit. P can't use own answers to interrogatories by D at trial. Have to testify.

f. AMENDMENT: Limits each party to 25 interrogatories.

3. RULES 27-32: DEPOSITIONS—Most controversial device. Usually done in attorney's office. Typically recorded by transcriber but new rule allows other methods, e.g. videotape. There is no judge and it's like court examination.

a. To set up deposition, serve on party to be deposed notice of deposition time and date (not done through court). This is an enforceable document against party—if they don't show they can be sanctioned and ordered to appear under RULE 37.

b. If notice of deposition is to a non-party, not enforceable under Rule 37, so you attach a subpoena which is a court order and provides the enforceability you need over non-party. (Same for production of documents).
   i. Old Rule—30 days notice
   ii. New Rule—No discovery can be sought/scheduled until Rule 26(f)—Meeting of the Parties—has occurred.

c. D can file under 26(c) a protective order to change location of deposition

d. To get witness from Kansas into Ga. court? Rule 45 (subpoena rule)—get a subpoena within the Kansas district where witness is located or within 100 miles of that district (Rule 4). Notice deposition within that same location. If in state court (no NW service of process)—look to procedures of state where witness is and comply with subpoena rules—most likely will take deposition in state where witness is located.

e. General Rule—attorney wanting an objection to an improper question, states objection on record. Witness still answers the question under the objection. If attorney does not object on record, it then is waived at trial. Only way to preserve objection is to get it on record.

4. RULE 35: MEDICAL EXAMINATION—Rule deals with a party in lawsuit wanting to force another party to undergo a medical examination and give information to them. "Privacy concerns." Can only get this by filing a court order and showing good cause for the request. Must be a legitimate issue of the case to get medical exam.

a. If examined party D gets copy of the report, so does P. What price does P pay in seeking copy of exam? —35(b)(ii)—waives privilege regarding testimony of every other person who has examined P in regard to same condition. Reciprocity—no longer any doctor/patient privilege.

b. Duty to Supplement Prior requests—Old Rule— fraught with mischief; had to determine whether response was complete when made, whether it was incorrect when made or became incorrect.

c. New Rule 26(e)—More straightforward. Must supplement if party learns that some material respect the information disclosed is incomplete or incorrect and if the additional information has not otherwise been made known during discovery process.

d. Any time you use out-of-court statement, it is hearsay. Preference for in-court oral statements because can't cross-examine a non-present witness. Can overcome this by dividing answers between party or non-party. If non-party, can't use out-of-court statements. Can get this testimony in, in limited circumstances:

    i.   If non-party testifies in court, and

    ii. Can use deposition, not to prove fact, but to impeach witness if they contradict a pre-existing statement. Use to attack credibility not as evidence-in-chief.

    iii. Can use deposition material if deponent is genuinely unavailable, e.g. dead

    iv. Can use deposition answer of party to suit as evidence-in-chief because their statements are not hearsay, but admissions. Also, party is usually present at trial.

D. MANAGING THE SCOPE AND BURDEN OF DIS-COVERY—Rule 26(b)—Old and new rule virtually identical.

  1. RULE 26(b)—You can ask for almost anything, includ-ing:

    a. Not privileged evidence, which is relevant to subject matter whether it relates to claim or defense. In addition, can ask for location of persons having knowledge of any discoverable matter.

    b. 26(b)(1)—Need not be admissible at trial, but should appear reasonably calculated to lead to discovery of admissible evidence.

    c. Can't ask for work product.

    d. 26(b)(1)—Identity of all persons having knowledge of any discoverable data.

    e. Davis v. Ross—Basic scope rule—Must ask—Is information reasonably calculated to lead to admis-sible evidence? Rule 26 says nothing about privacy limitations (only privileged) but court implies it. Court has discretion to limit disclosure under Rule 26 based on privacy concerns.

    f. 26(b)(4)—Discovery of Other Side's Experts— Threshold Question—Is expert going to testify at trial? If expert will testify at trial then opposing party can get interrogatories with report of their findings and opinions. Old Rule—must make special motion to court to compel a deposition—not automatically entitled to a deposition.

    g. If non-testifying expert there is no discovery available unless exceptional circumstances. This is considered work product. Exceptional circumstance, e.g. narrow field with only one expert so both parties are forced to share.

    h. NEW RULE—Allowed to depose testifying experts. Same rules for non-testifying experts.

        i. With testifying experts—all written information is now obtained under mandatory disclosure provision—not a discovery procedure. Deposition is still done through discovery.

        ii. Distinguishes between expert at trial due to expertise and expert that was eyewitness. If eyewitness, not subject to expert rules and normal discovery rules are used.

E. EXEMPTIONS FROM DISCOVERY

    1. Hickman v. Taylor—exception case. Rule 26—even if information is relevant, can't discover it if it's privileged. New privilege—WORK PRODUCT (can still get work product if you can prove substantial need and inability to get information yourself).

    2. WORK PRODUCT—Oral, written, and tangible items gained in anticipation of trial. Information gathered, developed, created in anticipation of trial. If did not

have privilege, other side would know everything the other side knows which could increase lying and decrease credibility at trial. Element of surprise is more compatible with search for truth.

3. Not just limited to efforts of gathering information in anticipation of trial by attorney, but anyone working in this vein, e.g. private investigator.

4. See Expert testimony (above).

F. ENFORCING THE DISCOVERY RULES—SANCTIONS —RULE 37—pertains to non-complying parties only.

1. Party that receives discovery request has three responses:
   a. Can go to court and seek permission not to respond to question. Rule 26(c)—protective order. Advantage: Don't engage in self-help.
   b. Engage in self-help by refusing to answer and put onus on other party to invoke court's powers.
   c. Not showing up at deposition or not sending interrogatories.

2. Rule 37(a)(2)(b) with Option #2—File Motion to Compel Answer—If court orders you to answer, you will also have to pay for cost of motion. If court orders you to answer and you don't then court has broader sanctions against you. Listed under Rule 37(c)(1)— circumstances triggering sanctions and 37(d)—list of "major league" sanctions

3. In option #3—discovering party can go directly to major league sanctions and can skip filing a motion to compel.
   a. Reasons to grant sanctions are reckless disregard, gross negligence, malevolence, willfulness.
   b. Major league sanctions include—Strike pleadings; establishment orders; disallow evidence; dismiss P's case with prejudice or default D's case.

4. NEW RULE—affects scope of Rule 37. Adds failure to make mandatory disclosures sanctionable (37(a)(2)(A).

5. 37(c)—court can do more than order disclosure, they can tag on sanctions. Can do this if three elements are met: Fails to disclose without substantial justification and not harmless.

6. Court is permitted (beyond order to disclose) to : 1) bar you from using non-disclosed evidence at trial and 2) On motion court may impose: attorney's fees, major league sanctions, and inform jury of failure to disclose.

7. Cine Forty-Second Street Theatre Corp. v. Allied Artists Pictures Corp.

7. RULES 26-37, AS AMENDED!!!

8. RULE 45—requires subpoenas to produce documents or inspection on particular date by non-party. Enumerate like Rule 34. Court can always sanction anyone who does not respond to court order subpoena. Contempt is inherent sanction power court has.

IV. DISPOSITION BEFORE TRIAL

A. SUMMARY JUDGMENT—Rule 56—advances to later stage in litigation, the screening out of baseless claims when we feel uncomfortable with level of facts. Summary judgment is like an advanced directed verdict motion.

1. RULE 56(c)—Moving party must show that there is no genuine issue as to any material fact and moving party is entitled to judgment as a matter of law. Maybe genuine issue—triable issue. As a matter of law, the jury has nothing to decide.

2. **Burden of Production**—Burden of producing certain level of evidence. Efficiency notion is within this concept. If didn't have this concept, would have to

pray that jury follows burden of persuasion instruction. Since this is not always the case, court will keep case from jury if insufficient evidence. No triable issue of fact generated due to insufficiency of evidence. Test for adequacy of evidence. Party that has burden of production does not necessarily have the burden of persuasion at trial.

3. **Burden of Persuasion**—Party's burden of convincing jury of the correctness of its position based on evidence. Civil standard is a preponderance of evidence. Criminal standard is beyond a reasonable doubt.

4. TEST
   a. Focuses on what if any burden Rule 56 places on moving party.
   b. Does non-moving party assume a burden?
   c. Is our assessment of the burdens of parties going to be influenced by which party has burden of production and persuasion of issues of fact at trial?

5. Adickes v. S.H. Kress & Co.—D moves for summary judgment claiming no genuine issue of material fact. Here, D did not do that but supplied affidavits to counter P's claim of civil rights violation. D failed to establish its burden and failed to foreclose the possibility of conspiracy even though D does not have this burden at trial. There is a burden of D to show absence of evidence of any genuine fact pointing to conspiracy. Court is looking for something affirmative indication absence of genuine issue.

6. Holding: Moving party must supply affirmative evidence that negates non-moving party's case on summary judgment motion where non-moving party has burden of production and persuasion at trial. Must show no issue for trial and no possibility of P's claim

prevailing based on evidence. Very high standard. Shows court's reluctance to grant S/J.

7. Moving party must do more to get court to scrutinize P's case in summary judgment as opposed to directed verdict because court is not as generous so early in timing of trial. S/J could be premature in that not all evidence is before court.

8. 20 days after filing of claim, party can move for S/J—Rule 56(a).

9. Rule 56(f) allows non-moving party to say—Hey, wait a minute! I have information but it can't be obtained right now. Give me more time for discovery.

10. <u>Celotex Corp. v. Catrett</u>—Supreme Court created 2 standards for moving party to get S/J:
   a. Affirmative evidence establishing that there is no genuine issue as to a material fact.
   b. D can point out the absence of evidence on P's side. Moves closer to directed verdict standard.
   c. Celotex used #2. Moving party can use record; roadmap of discovery to show that P has had ample time and no genuine issue has surfaced.
   d. If moving party (without burden of production) wants to use standard #2, they must aggressively pursue, discover, e.g. depose P's witnesses, etc. Moving party must make sure a record is generated for the court to review.
   e. 56(e)—When motion is made and supported as provided, an adverse party may not rely only on denial but must set forth specific facts showing there is an absence of a genuine issue of fact.
   f. P can't use absence of evidence standard because when P is moving party they also hold the burden of production and persuasion at trial. Can't shift that burden to D.

B. MEETING THE BURDEN OF PRODUCTION: DETER-
MINING THE APPROPRIATE STANDARD

   1. <u>Arnstein v. Porter</u>—Holding: P can avoid S/J by
   raising issues of moving party's credibility without any
   affirmative evidence. Anti-S/J approach.

   2. <u>Dyer v. MacDougall</u>—Court says that it is not enough
   for P to prove that credibility of witnesses could make
   his case. You need to prove your case by providing
   evidence; not by showing other side has not met burden
   to negate. Can't go to trial based on credibility of D's
   witnesses and must provide affirmative evidence—true
   if P has burden at trial.

   3. Where there is very little tangible fact because case
   turns on subjective motivation of party it is probably
   easier to use credibility as a reason to allow trial to
   occur.

   4. Sometimes procedural rules don't work clearly and
   results are based on underlying substantive issue.
   Substantive law influences procedure.

   5. RULE 56

V. **TRIAL**

   A. Pretrial conference

   B. Settlement promotion using court-administered simulated
   substitutes for full trial

      1. summary jury trial

      2. court-annexed arbitration

   C. Phases of a trial

      1. jury selection

      2. opening statements

      3. presentation of evidence

4. argument

5. instructions

6. jury deliveration and verdict

7. post-trial motions and judgment

8. rule 16, as amended!!!

D. Seventh Amendment Right to jury Trial—Right to jury trial shall be preserved. Since amendment says preserved, must know difference between law and equity as they were separate at time amendment was enacted.

1. Very important who will be finder of facts. Juries deliberate in secret, don't run through rationale of decision. In certain cases, result will be different depending on whether judge or jury is trier of fact.

2. Problem in modern day in applying historical test because:

   a. There are new substantive claims that did not exist back at common law.

   b. Merger between courts of equity and law. Procedural changes, e.g. Federal rules now exist, e.g. Joinder—ability to file multiple claims in one proceeding and joining claims that were formally filed under separate court systems.

3. Beacon Theatres, Inc. v. Westover—Holding: If there are multiple claims in lawsuit and one of the claims is in law and one in equity, the legal claim is tried first. True if the two claims have factual overlap. S/C holds that jury trial is warranted because equity was an extreme remedy at C/L. Want to err on side of jury trial.

   i. If claims have nothing to do with each other then you don't care which is heard first. But if common issue, and equity claim is tried first by judge, it may foreclose the jury from finding on common issues in law claim, e.g. res judicata, collateral estoppel.

ii. Defines right of jury trial as preserving something from 1791.

4. <u>Dairy Queen, Inc. v. Wood</u>—Clean-up doctrine—When go into equity court and resolve issues and there is an incidental legal issue, it is resolved by the equity court. Under historical test—no jury trial because equity court would clean up consequential legal issue. With merger, however, now no need for equity claim to be heard first. This case—the height of the court's desire for jury trial.

5. <u>Ross v. Bernhard</u>—Derivative suits were recognized in equity courts at C/L. Derivative suit was procedural device to get into equity court; however, now that courts have merged it is not necessary. Must look beyond equitable procedural device to the underlying issue. In this case, the underlying issue was a legal claim so there is a right to jury trial.

6. <u>Curtis v. Loether</u>—Title VII is more like a restitution remedy. Fair representation claim—legal claim because it causes harm to the employee to go to court and costs employee. The union didn't hold back pay so they didn't profit. Union is not making restitution but paying employee damages. This is different from Terry where back pay was held by company—more like restitution.

7. Applying two-part test:
   a. Housing discrimination claim is like a C/L tort claim—legal cause of action;
   b. Remedy was punitive—law remedy—jury trial proper.

E. Right to jury trial in statutorily-created administrative proceedings

   1. <u>Teamsters Local No. 391 v. Terry</u>—Test:
      a. Find closest common law claim to this claim. If this claim is in law then jury trial.

b. Look at nature of relief sought.

c. What if remedy is determined through administrative body before it can go to Court of Appeals? Legislature establishes federal agency which is within their right. Congress can manipulate remedy to keep juries out of case.

d. Why do we allow Congress to take public law claims out of courts and into administrative agencies but not private claims? Administrative agencies—Congress can only regulate for general welfare and in public domain. Congress may avoid 7th amendment if they had authority to create administrative tribunal. When they have power to set up agency, as an incidence, they have power to assign adjudicating duties to that agency.

2. 14th Amendment does not cover 7th amendment so if state court wants to operate differently they can. However, need to look at state constitution to see how jury trial works.

3. Right to jury trial is waivable. Must demand the right—Rule 38. If don't invoke it you lose it.

4. Any party can invoke a jury trial

5. In Ga., right to trial by jury is automatic, don't have to demand it .

6. Changing jury characteristics does not violate 7th amendment.

7. How do jury and law relate to each other?

a. Jury selection—make sure jury compatible with due process. Try to reduce biases.

b. Law of evidence—insulates jury as to what information they may hear;

c. Jury instructions—standard to be used, etc.

8. Ultimate way to control jury is to take case away from them.

F. Judicial control of verdict

   1. Directed verdict and judgment NOV

   2. RULE 50—D can move for directed verdict at end of P's case or at end of all evidence.

      a. Contrasting Directed Verdict and Judgment NOV

   3. RULE 50 (a)- DIRECTED VERDICT—tests legal sufficiency of P's production. Has P provided enough evidence to send to jury? Could reasonable person find for P based on evidence provided? Tests whether P has met their burden of production where a jury (reasonable person) could find for P. New rule—now called Judgment as a matter of law

   4. RULE 50(b)—JUDGMENT NOV—New rule now called renewal of judgment as a matter of law. Substantively there is not difference between DV and JNOV. JNOV—deferred DV motion. One may not move for JNOV unless previously moved for DV at close of all evidence.

      a. When court denies motion for D.V. at end of trial, you are renewing it after the jury rules—JNOV.

      b. Must move for JNOV within 10 days of entry of judgment.

      c. Standards of Evidence Necessary to Overcome Motion for Directed Verdict:
         i. Mere Scintilla—not usually enough anymore. The more conjecture needed for jury to find for P—the more uncomfortable the court gets in sending case to jury.
         ii. Substantial Evidence

d. <u>Lavender v. Kurn</u>—substance influences procedure! Two sub-sets of Directed Verdict Standard:
   i. View evidence in light most favorable to non-moving party.
   ii. Not the court's function to weigh competing evidence or credibility of witness. This is jury question.
e. When D moves at end of all evidence, what role does D's evidence take? Courts generally hold that you can consider aspects of D's case that were unimpeached if directed verdict moved for at end of case. Considers P's evidence in light most favorable to P and any unimpeached or uncontradicted evidence of D.

5. MOTION FOR NEW TRIAL—Post-trial motion. Verdict was tainted in some way so asking court to take judgment away and start all over. Rule 50 (b)
   a. What would entitle a verdict loser to a new trial?
      i. Where verdict tainted due to court's procedural error
         1. allows evidence in that should have been left out
         2. improper instructions to jury
         3. Doesn't matter whether we appeal directly.
      ii. Don't have to preserve new trial.
   b. Where verdict is contrary to manifest weight of evidence. Here, not saying case is legally insufficient but asking judge to act as 13th juror. Here judge can weigh evidence and credibility. Saying that evidence is lopsided thus motion is discretionary.
   c. If T/C grants motion for new trial, it is unappealable because you are getting a new trial and it's not a final judgment.

d. If T/C denies motion for new trial, appealable because it is a final decision.

e. Hard to get appellate court to reverse T/C because they saw all the evidence.

f. Neely case—When a verdict loser loses and thinks lost unjustly they will want to file a JNOV But even if you think that evidence is legally sufficient the manifest weight of the evidence still should have been in D's favor, then file motion for a new trial in the alternative.

CONTRACTS

I. CONTRACTS

A. DEFINITIONS

1. CONTRACT—Legally enforceable promise that has an exchange; Set of promises; Mutuality of obligations.
2. BARGAIN THEORY OF CONTRACTS—One promise exchanged for another; Objective is to make the innocent party whole. Compensatory only.
3. PROMISE—commitment to perform some future act
4. PROMISOR—person who breaches
5. PROMISEE—injured party
6. PERFORMANCE— when both parties keep promises
7. BREACH—promisor has not kept his promise
8. EXCHANGE—CONSIDERATION; exchange of promises
9. RECISSION—Mutual agreement to cancel contract
10. COVENANT—term of contract

B. ELEMENTS OF CONTRACT

1. OFFER—promise to do something
2. ACCEPTANCE—promise to comply with offer
3. CONSIDERATION—an exchange; must be induced by offer which induces acceptance
4. MUST HAVE definiteness, assent, intent to create contract

C. TWO TYPES OF CONTRACTS

1. UNILATERAL—a promise for performance, can be withdrawn anytime up until performance
2. BILATERAL—a promise for a promise

D. IMPLIED TERMS IN EVERY CONTRACT

1. Good faith
2. Reasonableness
3. Best efforts
4. Trade usage and custom of trade
5. Fair dealing
6. Contract not against public policy
7. Contract not unconscionable

II. CAPACITY—looks at status of parties; person must have power or capacity to contract for contract to be valid.

A. CONTRACTS

1. VOIDABLE CONTRACT—A contract is valid unless option is taken to void it.
2. VOID CONTRACT—there never was a contract, was invalid at the outset.
3. DISAFFIRM A CONTRACT—action to void contract, give it back.

B. IMMATURITY—a contract with a minor is voidable by minor; minor may disaffirm contact at any time while still minor; when minor disaffirms, only requirement is that he return the item that is subject of contract; condition of item is irrelevant (could get totaled car back and minor could get money back!).

1. EXCEPTIONS
   a. NECESSITY—subjective standard; depends on facts and circumstances of each case; to determine whether subject matter is necessity courts look at:
      i. Social position
      ii. Social status
      iii. Wealth
      iv. Peers

     v. Neighborhood.

    vi. Anything that others in minor's circle have is considered a necessity.

   vii. Minor accountable for reasonable value of any necessity. Contracts for necessity are not voidable.

  b. EMANCIPATED MINOR—renunciation of parental duties; can be severed by parents or minor; marriage makes minor emancipated; majority of courts say that minor can still disaffirm as long as it's not a contract for necessity; minority of courts say they can't.

2. RATIFICATION

  a. When minor enters contract, it can be disaffirmed at any time, however when reaches age of majority, minor has reasonable time to disaffirm before his action ratifies contract.

  b. Ratification is a manifestation of the intent to be bound.

  c. Occurs when person has committed any act which indicates that the person is treating the contract as if it exists, includes:

    i. damaging subject of contract

    ii. improving subject of contract.

  d. Have reasonable time to disaffirm before ratification; reasonableness is fact specific.

  e. Minor can't ratify contract; nothing minor does ratifies contract including damaging subject of contract.

  f. Ratification is a defense to disaffirment.

C. MENTAL INCAPACITY—How tell? How do those close to him treat him? Expert testimony.

1. Incapacitated person's rights in regard to contract

a. Person who is judged to be mentally incompetent has the right to disaffirm or void a contract.

b. They may void the contract; however, they must pay restitution for value of subject of contract. Must pay amount of enrichment or amount of benefit conferred on him or damage caused to subject of contract.

2. TESTS TO DETERMINE MENTAL INCAPACITY

a. COGNITIVE TEST—Whether person knows or understands the nature and consequences of his actions; whether person knows or understands the nature and consequences of the contract.

   i. Disadvantages: Person may understand the nature of contract but be so mentally affected they can't control their actions (schizophrenic).

   ii. Person can appear competent and court can still decide they are mentally incompetent which is unfair to other party who could not tell.

b. MODERN TEST—person claiming to be mentally incompetent must

   i. show they are unable to act in a reasonable manner and

   ii. other party must know about the condition and inabilities of the person.

c. OTHER DETERMINANTS—Courts infer competence from facts and consequences of case, not just medical testimony. Courts look at how person acted and how people who knew him best treated him.

D. INCAPACITY DUE TO ALCOHOL ABUSE—Majority view—it's irrelevant if mental incompetence is self-induced; if other party knows about it then the contract is voidable. Minority view—some jurisdictions exclude drunkenness to put burden on drunkard, not other party. Some courts say that drug impairment is worse because it can lead to mental incapacity.

III. FORMATION

A. ASK

   1. Has there been a promise?

   2. Has there been a detriment?

   3. Has detriment been exchanged for promise and vice versa?

B. THE OFFER—a promise or commitment to do or refrain from doing something in the future; inherent in commitment is the intent to be bound. Check : Is it illusory?

   1. TERMS

      a. OFFEROR—Master of his offer; has full power which he transfers to offeree. When you make an offer you confer upon another the power to create a contract.

      b. OBJECTIVE THEORY OF OFFER—Look to actions of offeror to determine whether a reasonable person in shoes of offeree would believe that an offer has been made. We assume person serious unless we knew or should have known that he wasn't.

      c. PROPOSALS—offers subject to approval.

      d. CONDITIONAL PROMISE—a promise to do something in future upon the happening of contingency. Not binding offer unless stated event occurs.

   2. TO DETERMINE OFFER—look at parties' intent; did they intend to be bound? Did person making offer intend to be bound? Did person accepting offer intend to be bound?

   3. GENERAL OFFERS—ADVERTISING

      a. An offer is a commitment to sell unless offer is advertisement and ad could lead to unlimited liability to merchant. QUALIFIED AD is an offer. UNQUALIFIED AD is an invitation to negotiate.

b. Ways to Retract—
   i. Make public retraction the same way offer was made.
   ii. Implicit in every public offer that specifies quantity is term first come, first served, which allows revocation.
c. Letter of intent—agreement to agree.

4. IRREVOCABLE OFFERS/OPTION CONTRACTS—
Offers are irrevocable pursuant to other contracts; contractors agree that offers they submit are irrevocable; contractors' bids are usually irrevocable.
   a. Elements:
      i. By contract, say it will be open for period of time
      ii. If someone relies on offer to their detriment and it would be unjust to let you revoke—Detrimental reliance.
   b. Irrevocable Offers can be rescinded when:
      i. Offeror made mistake that was not a neglect of legal duty.
      ii. Enforcement would be unconscionable—grossly unfair.
      iii. Offeree can be placed in status quo ante without hardship or expense.
   c. If breach irrevocable offer—argue no consideration; if spent money but no contract, argue promissory estoppel.

5. COMMUNICATIONS THAT DON'T CONSTITUTE OFFER—under UCC 2-207
   a. Price inquiries
   b. General inquiries
   c. Price quote
   d. Advertisements, except if terms are specific, e.g. first come, first served . . . only ten left . . .)

6. REASONABLE TIME STANDARD—Offer is good for reasonable time determined by facts and circumstances of case.

7. WAYS TO TERMINATE OFFER
   a. REVOCATION
      i. Must take place before acceptance
      ii. Words used; such as I revoke, I withdraw
      iii. Conduct—any act inconsistent with offer is revocation of offer
      iv. Effective when received by offeree, once a person knows of revocation, they can no longer accept.
      v. When offeree knows or should have known that offer has been revoked, no longer can accept.
      vi. If offeree does not know about revocation, then there is a breach and offeree can sue for damages or performance.
   b. DEATH OR INCAPACITY
      i. Must take place before acceptance
      ii. Death terminates offer automatically
      iii. Mental incapacity terminates offer automatically
      iv. Physical incapacity terminates offer if physical performance is required in contract.
      v. If there is a contract already, death or incapacity will not terminate contract.
      vi. Offeree's knowledge of death is irrelevant.
   c. LAPSE OF OFFER—Expires by its terms or time limit set by offeror; if no express time, then offer expires at reasonable time; subjective; telephone offers usually lapse at end of call; face-to-face meeting offers usually lapse at end of meeting.
   d. REJECTION
      i. Simple rejection—I reject . . . no thanks.
      ii. Implied by conduct—actions which are inconsistent with intention to accept the offer.

   iii. Counteroffer—acceptance doesn't match the terms; once offeree rejects, can't take offer back.

   iv. Way to negotiate without rejecting offer—I'll consider that, now will you consider this? Must let other party know that you are not intending to reject their offer.

  8. THINGS THAT CAN HAPPEN TO OFFER

   a. lapse

   b. be revoked

   c. be rejected

   d. be accepted.

 C. ACCEPTANCE—an agreement to comply with or perform the terms of the offer; Also called mutuality, meeting of the minds, assent; without assent there is no contract.

  1. ASSENT—Manifestation of agreement by words, conduct, or action; mutuality; meeting of the minds.

  2. REQUIREMENTS TO HAVE ACCEPTANCE

   a. There must be an expression of assent—a commitment to comply with the terms of the offer; an expression of assent may be expressed

    i. orally

    ii. in writing

    iii. implied or inferred by conduct. Irrelevant what real unexpressed state of mind of parties is.

   b. Acceptance must be unconditional—must be last step in contract

   c. Acceptance must be identical to the offer

    i. MIRROR IMAGE RULE—Acceptance must mirror the offer; if it alters it at all, it is a counteroffer not an acceptance.

    ii. COUNTEROFFER—an acceptance that does not comply with the terms of the offer, but is a commitment to offer.

iii. PROPOSALS—offers that are deficient, subject to approval

d. What happens if acceptance not made but person who could have relied on that offer? Courts say if it's unjust to require the acceptance be made in return for the offer, we will convert offer into irrevocable offer (option contract) therefore can recover expectancy damages.

3. TEST TO DETERMINE ASSENT
   a. Is there a promise or commitment?
   b. Have the parties indicated an intent to be bound (assent)?
   c. If one manifests an intent to assent from view of reasonable person then there is assent unless the other party knew or should have known that other party was not serious.

4. DEFINITENESS—if terms of offer are not definite, then there is no assent and promise is unenforceable. Can be used as a defense to enforcement. Reliance on indefinite promise is not justified. Reasonableness and good faith are definite terms of contract. Reasonableness is fact-specific. Must be definite output or quantity.

5. UCC—ARTICLE 2—governs sale of foods; if offer is for sale of goods, acceptance does not have to mirror the offer. BATTLE OF THE FORMS!
   a. UCC 2-207 (1-3) states that an acceptance is treated as assent even if it is different from offer when
      i. The parties indicate an intent to be bound
      ii. Looks at parties' conduct for expression of acceptance.
   b. Additional terms are part of contract unless
      i. Offer expressly limits terms to acceptance of offer

      ii. Additional terms do not materially alter contract

     iii. Notification of objections.

  c. KNOCKOUT RULE—if transaction is completed without assent to terms, UCC 2-207 says that contract is complete. Terms are deemed to be whatever the parties agreed on, and the conflicting terms are knocked out and replaced with UCC provisions.

  d. FALLOUT RULE—I—If transaction is completed without assent to terms, UCC 2-207 says that contract is complete. Additional terms are construed as proposals and not as part of contract. Whichever term was submitted first stays in and the second term falls out. Original terms control. Based on theory that offeror is master of the offer.

  e. FALLOUT RULE—II—Some courts have original term fallout and second term control. Based on theory that they performed contract and that constitutes acceptance of the term.

D. CONSIDERATION—An exchange of one promise for another promise; an exchange of a promise for a legal detriment; DETRIMENT—doing something you don't have to do or not doing something you have a legal right to do. Can be promise, action, or inaction. If there is no exchange, there is no consideration and therefore, no contract. Benefit not necessary to have consideration.

  1. ELEMENTS OF CONSIDERATION

    a. Promisee must suffer a legal detriment; to forego cocaine is not detriment because not a legal right.

    b. Detriment must induce promise.

    c. Promise must induce detriment.

    d. Detriment does not have to be equal to the promise.

  2. UNENFORCEABLE PROMISES—a promise is a commitment to perform some future act.

a. ILLUSORY PROMISE—Promise with no commitment; not definite as to time. Does not create an obligation. When promise seems illusory, must ask:
   i. Is there reasonableness?
   ii. Is there good faith? An unrestricted right to terminate contract is illusory; courts are reluctant to find promise illusory unless promisor can withdraw without any restrictions. Unrestricted right to terminate is not commitment therefore illusory. Look for restrictions in right to terminate.
   iii. How to determine reasonableness in termination?
      a. If restriction is unreasonable because it's inane, e.g., when Martians land
      b. If reasonable, then upheld.
b. GRATUITOUS PROMISE—Promise made by one who has not received consideration for it. A promise that does not seek any detriment. Past performance can not count as consideration to current promise. A gift is a gratuitous promise. Unenforceable.
c. MORAL OBLIGATION—There is no exchange; small number of jurisdictions say moral obligation does render promise enforceable when there is a benefit conferred; Not recognized by most courts, e.g., been loyal employee. Unenforceable generally, promise did not induce detriment.
d. PAST CONSIDERATION—promise to do something in exchange for something already done. There is no exchange and promise is unenforceable. Did not induce detriment.
e. PRE-EXISTING DUTY—promise to do something in exchange for something you are already committed to do. A promise to pay additional amount to induce one to do what they are already contractually obligated to do. No consideration—no detriment.

    i. Exception in restatement—can be enforceable when the change in contract is fair and equitable under the circumstances and circumstances were unanticipated at the time the contract was made.

    ii. Weakness of Rule—doesn't distinguish between opportunistic and greedy party and the legitimate party who wants to renegotiate because of unforeseen circumstances. Also inconsistent use of recission, remedy, and fairness.

3. BASIS FOR RECOVERY ON PROMISE—Ways to enforce promise.

  a. CONSIDERATION (see above)

  b. RELIANCE—PROMISSORY ESTOPPEL (DETRIMENTAL RELIANCE)—When a person relies on a promise to their detriment with no consideration. A promise is made and the promisor is estopped from denying the promise because promisee relied on it.

  c. IMPORTANT—requires a promise; can't use if promise is illusory; motivation of promisor is irrelevant.

    i. ELEMENTS

      a. Did promisee reasonably rely or justifiably rely on promise? Look at whether he acted or not acted because of promise and was that action or inaction justifiable. Justifiable reliance is a reasonable-person standard. Promisee must suffer detriment in reliance of promise.

      b. The promisor must have reasonable expectation that promise will be relied on by promisee. Promisor must reasonably expect promisee to act or not act in reliance of promise.

      c. Can injustice be avoided only by enforcement of promise—transcendental component?

ii. UNILATERAL CONTRACTS—This type of offer seeks performance; contract is only good when contract is performed; neither party is bound until contract is performed; can only be accepted by conduct, not bound by promise; promise can be revoked anytime before acceptance. Three views:

a. Master of Offer—if offer seeks performance, then offeror is not bound until performance is performed and offeror can revoke anytime until then. Oldest and traditional view; not really fair; remember Spike at door with Stephen's revoking

b. Even though offer seeks performance, contract arises when offeree starts to perform. Offer is accepted once performance is begun; not fair because offeror is bound but offeree isn't.

c. Once offeree begins to perform, offer becomes irrevocable. There is not a contract, however offer can't be revoked.

d. TENDER OF PERFORMANCE—Offer to perform, coupled with readiness, willingness, and ability to perform.

d. RESTITUTION—as cause of action rather than remedy; really means act of restoring actual money or property or equivalent value of property to their rightful owner. Looks at amount by which party was enriched. IMPLIED PROMISE, QUASI-CONTRACT—No promise made, but there is consensual transaction. Promise to pay can be inferred from circumstances. UNJUST ENRICHMENT—theory of recovery; party is unjustly enriched unless they are required to return to rightful owner money or property to give them restitution. Requires consent.

i. ELEMENTS:
   a. When someone confers a benefit on you and
   b. it would be unjust for you to retain benefit without paying for it.
ii. DEFENSES:
   a. The benefit was gratuitously conferred with no expectation of payment,
   b. The benefit was subject of contract (there is no contract with restitution causes),
   c. Benefit is not calculable,
   d. Benefit was conferred officiously—by good Samaritan or intermeddler. (e.g., rendering emergency medical aid). As public policy matter however, may imply promise to encourage Drs. to assist—offset malpractice risks.
iii. DAMAGES:
   a. Prospective of Promisee—amount of payment would be cost of providing benefit, e.g., paint and labor
   b. Prospective of Promisor—Look at benefit conferred; value of what was received, b) (value of services rendered) or, c) increased value to promisor (difference in value of item before service and after service was rendered).

4. IN GENERAL
   a. A promise to not file a lawsuit is consideration when:
      i. you act in good faith; believe that claim is valid and that have basis to file claim (subjective element)
      ii. Must have a claim based in law; there must in fact be a basis to file claim (objective element)

IV. MISCELLANEOUS TYPES OF CONTRACTS

A. REQUIREMENTS CONTRACT—a contract where one party is obligated to supply all the goods that the other party might require. Enforceable, not illusory despite the fact that one party can say, I don't need any.

B. OUTPUT CONTRACT—Contract where one party is required to purchase everything the other party produces. Enforceable, not illusory despite fact that one party can say I haven't produced any.

C. OPTION CONTRACT/IRREVOCABLE OFFER— Offeror can't sell without offeree getting first crack at offer; gives offeree exclusivity and right of first refusal; enforceable if supported by consideration; UCC 2-205—a firm offer option contract is enforceable without consideration, if it is in writing.

V. STATUTE OF FRAUDS—Some contracts, in order to be enforceable, must be in writing; statute only deals with enforceability; does not require a signed contract, only that there be some writing that evidences a contract. Just because a contract is not enforceable under Statute, does not mean there is not recovery—there is still Unjust Enrichment and Detrimental Reliance!!!

A. CONTRACTS COVERED BY STATUTE OF FRAUDS—Ask: Must these contracts be in writing in order to be enforceable?

1. Contract by executor or administrator—contract must be in writing any time executor promises to pay debt of decedent out of executor's own money.

2. Suretyship—promise to pay debt of another; Statute applies where both original debtor and surety become obligated on debt at same time; does not apply where creditor extinguishes one debt for another; only applies

where there are two debts owed the creditor—one by original debtor and one by surety; does not apply if original debtor and surety already have independent liability to the creditor (e.g. partnership, partner already liable for debts of partner).

3. MAIN PURPOSE or Leading Object Rule—despite suretyship provision, if main purpose of making promise is to benefit surety, not the promisor, then it is not within the Statute.

4. Contract in consideration of marriage—not enforceable unless in writing

5. Contract for Sale of Interest in Land—any promise to create or transfer an interest in land must be in writing. Includes lease if for more than a year.

6. Contract Not To Be Performed Within One Year—Reference points are time of making contract and time of performance. If time of performance is more than a year after time of making contract, it must be in writing under Statute. If it is possible that contract can be performed in a year, even if it's not probable, it does not fall within Statute.

B. UNILATERAL CONTRACTS AND STATUTE OF FRAUDS—Where performance is acceptance, the time of contract and the time of performance are simultaneous, therefore unilateral contracts are not within the Statute.

C. UCC AND STATUTE OF FRAUDS—UCC 2-201 state that when there is a contract for more than $500 there must be some writing evidencing contract and writing must be signed by person who breached. Only applies to contracts between merchants.

1. 2-201 (2) states that a writing signed by D isn't necessary to satisfy Statute when:

a. There is a confirmation of contract signed by person who sent the confirmation and,

b. Confirmation is sufficient to bind the sender

c. Confirmation is received

d. Recipient knows or has reason to know what is in the confirmation

e. Recipient doesn't object to confirmation within ten days, will be considered acceptance.

2. Court looks at:

a. Would either party be prejudiced if document is ruled not to be a document and

b. actions of parties.

3. 2-207 relieves merchants of having to have writing signed by person who is charged with breach.

D. DEFENSES TO STATUTE OF FRAUDS—Statute of Frauds recognizes a contract, no matter if it is unenforceable.

1. UNJUST ENRICHMENT—Can overcome Statute when party received benefit and it would be unjust for them to invoke statute. Party is then estopped from invoking Statute as defense against breach. As defense of Statute, not cause of action. Some courts require third element of unconscionable injury.

2. PROMISSORY ESTOPPEL—can overcome Statute when all elements for promissory estoppel are met and there is an unconscionable injury. Promissory estoppel makes Statute impotent, so courts added the element of unconscionable injury. Some courts say that Promissory Estoppel is enough even without unconscionability element.

3. UCC 2-201 (3)—admitting to contract is defense to Statute.

4. UCC 1-103 provides that principle of estoppel is all through or permeates the code unless provision says to the contrary. 2-201 does not say you can't use estoppel.

VI. POLICING THE BARGAIN—defenses to breach of contract claims. Purpose is to protect an agreement against unfairness.

A. Court looks at:

1. Status of parties—capacity

2. Substance of bargain—is bargain itself fair or unfair

3. Behavior of parties—how parties acted during bargaining process.

4. Defenses To Enforcement of Promise include: Maturity; Mental Incapacity; Duress; Pre-existing Duty Rule; Unfairness if equity relief is sought; Accord and Satisfaction.

5. When contract appears to be contract on its face ask:

   a. Is it consistent with public policy?

   b. Is it unconscionable?

   c. Was there assent? Was it reasonable for someone in that position to understand it? Courts look at level of education, economic level, etc.

B. DEFENSES TO ENFORCEMENT OF CONTRACTS OR AVOID PROMISE—Goes to both entire contract or a provision.

1. When provision ruled unenforceable, the court can:

   a. Refuse to enforce contact altogether

   b. Delete offending provision

   c. Modify offending provision so it adheres to standards

   d. Can reformulate provision so adheres to standards.

2. MENTAL INCAPACITY

3. MINORITY STATUS

4. PRE-EXISTING DUTY RULE

5. RECOVERY IN EQUITY—FAIRNESS—courts start with presumptions
   a. restrictions on land are bad
   b. if contract is oppressive, it's bad (unequal bargaining power),
   c. if contract is unfair, it is bad. Look at consideration as adequate, not sufficient. Looks at two competing theories:
      i. If contract unfair at any point, equity not appropriate
      ii. Looks at contract's fairness at time it was made.

6. ACCORD AND SATISFACTION—When there is a dispute and one party sends money in satisfaction of claim and other party agrees (accords)—there is an agreement. Only available when amount owed is in dispute; payment has to be sent in satisfaction of disputed amount. Must show mutuality. Don't need to cash check to have accord, just hold it for a reasonable time.

7. UNCONSCIONABILITY—That which shocks the conscience and offends sense of decency. Purpose is to prevent oppression, unfair surprise.
   a. ELEMENTS:
      i. Contract must be unfair and one-sided
      ii. There must be an inequality of bargaining power (looks to economic status of parties, most courts take position that if poor, you have no bargaining power; there will always be inequality, question is how much? This element will usually be met.)

      iii. There must be an absence of meaningful choice. Same elements for ADHESION CONTRACT. Adhesion contract also has elements of AS-SENT.

      iv. DRAGNET CLAUSE—security interest on all furniture purchases until pay off everything. Have right to take it all back.

  b. In general—Gross inequality of bargaining power will overcome element of meaningful choice. The greater the inequality, the less court will look at meaningful choice. When meaningful choice drops because of bargaining power disparity, only element court looks at is unfairness.

8. PUBLIC POLICY—based on protecting public; when the contract or any provision thereof violates public policy to extent that contract conflicts with public interests. Does contract harm public? If lose this argument, try unconscionability.

  a. ELEMENTS—

      i. Contract is to induce public official to act in certain manner

      ii. Contract is to do illegal act

      iii. Contract involves collusive bidding

      iv. Contract is against public policy

9. ILLEGAL CONTRACT—If contract is for illegal activity before contract is formed, it never was contract. Can't contract for illegal act or activity. If subject of contract becomes illegal after contract is formed, the contract becomes void.

10. DURESS

  a. DEFINITION—a serious, grave, and wrongful threat that forces you to do something against your will. Usually involves some type of violence. Used as a defense to breach-of-contract claim. Threat to file lawsuit is not duress because it is not wrongful. Wrongful must be element of duress.

b. ECONOMIC DURESS— a wrongful threat to withhold needful goods. Needful is something that is required to meet a contract.

c. Elements:
   i. <u>Wrongful</u> withholding of needful goods;
   ii. Can't be obtained elsewhere;
   iii. Remedy for breach is inadequate.

d. These elements look at victim's position. Fourth element added—Is duressor acting wrongfully?

e. Defense of economic duress must be asserted at earliest possible opportunity.

11. MISREPRESENTATION—When party has duty to disclose and doesn't or party misrepresents facts. A willful intent to deceive.

a. ELEMENTS:
   i. A false representation of existing or past fact
   ii. The misrepresentation must be material, substantial, important.
   iii. Must be fraudulent—a willful intent to deceive
   iv. Must have reliance on misrepresentation— someone must justifiably rely on misrepresentation when they entered contract.
   v. Misrepresentation must be a fact, not an opinion—aesthetics are opinions, value is opinion. To determine difference between fact and opinion, courts look at expertise of person making statement, how specific or particular or general the statement is (more general, the more likely it is an opinion), and the formality of the statement (oral tend to be opinions, written tend to be facts).

b. FALSE REPRESENTATION OF THE LAW—not basis for rescission because people are presumed to know the law (ignorance is no excuse). Exception is if person falsely representing law is a lawyer or a fiduciary in position of trust.

12. MISTAKE—an erroneous belief about a material fact, no intent to deceive.
  a. MUTUAL MISTAKE—occurs when both parties
    i. Mistake goes to basic assumption of contract.
    ii. Has material effect on consideration (grossly inadequate)
    iii. Neither party making mistake indicated that they would bear the burden of loss (no provision made for burden)
    iv. Neither party is to blame for mistake, no one is at fault. In contracts, party must affirmatively do something to be blameworthy. Issue: did you cause the mistake, not could you have avoided the mistake. Person is responsible for mistake when they knew or should have known about it, they are charged with knowledge of subject.
  b. UNILATERAL MISTAKE—occurs when one party knows of the other party's mistake. Generally can't be rescinded unless:
    i. Mistake is known by other party, they know you are making a mistake.
    ii. Party who knows the truth is responsible for the belief of the other party.
    iii. Enforcing the contract would be unconscionable or grossly unfair.
  c. CAVEAT EMPTOR—Duty to disclose. In general, the buyer must beware:
    i. That there is no duty to disclose when there is no special relationship between the parties (e.g., familial, fiduciary); no false representation;

haven't prevented you from discovery; haven't made a partial disclosure (if you do, then you must make a full disclosure).

    ii. There is a duty to disclose where there is a special relationship; there is partial disclosure; there is a mistaken basic assumption on material, substantial factor (something you knew that other party was relying on); there is special knowledge (not readily available to other party).

13. NO ASSENT—Contract is unenforceable because there was no real assent; no true agreement to terms.

  a. ELEMENTS

    i. Would reasonable person see the contract or provision, or something other than a contract, e.g., parking stub? Would reasonable person understand contract or provision?

    ii. Was the provision or contract brought to the attention of the other party? Was there notice? Was the provision buried in fine print or did it have a misnamed term?

    iii. Was there an opportunity to accept or reject the contract or provision? ADHESION CONTRACT—take it or leave it.

  b. To determine adhesion contract, courts look at:

    i. Education level—Is it reasonable for this person to understand?

    ii. Economic level—Could this person buy elsewhere, goes to meaningful choice issue.

  c. UCC 2-719 (2)—When contract remedy fails at its essential purpose, (when circumstances cause an exclusive or limited remedy to fail), the provision is unenforceable and the code will govern the contract. Must look at what is the essential purpose of provision (buyer and seller may have differing views).

d. UCC 2-314 and 2-315—Implied Warranty of Mer-
chantability—states that products sold must be
sellable. To defend against this seller can
  i. Expressly disclaim all warranties or
 ii. Offer a minimum remedy for any warranty
     claim. Warrants that goods are merchantable.
iii. Seller can expressly state no warranties so then
     court will not imply one. Or can offer limited
     warranty.

VII. BREACH OF CONTRACT—an enforceable promise that
the promisor refuses to keep; promisor breaches the contract.
PURPOSE OF CONTRACT LAW—to enforce promises; if
promise is not kept, to make the innocent party whole. Not
looking to punish the breaching party (no punitive damages in
contract law).

A. DAMAGE REMEDIES FOR BREACH—Burden of proof
   is on promisee; can only recover what you lost; damages
   must be FORESEEABLE; damages can't be SPECULA-
   TIVE; promisee must prove them within a degree of
   certainty; can claim more than one type of damage.

   1. RESTITUTION DAMAGES—Restores innocent party
      the benefit he conferred; looks at what promisor has
      gained; enables promisee to get his money back.

   2. RELIANCE DAMAGES—Returns promisee to status
      quo ante; puts promisee in position he was in before
      contract was made; Looks at what promisee lost; looks
      at detriment promisee incurred. Includes restitution
      damages.

   3. EXPECTANCY DAMAGES—Puts promisee in posi-
      tion would have been in had contract been performed;
      looks at what could the promisee have gained; usually
      sought when promisee can prove lost profits.

B. EQUITABLE REMEDIES FOR BREACH—Only available when money will not make person whole; subject of promise is unique (heirloom, land); when there is an inability to COVER for sale of goods at reasonable price; COVER only used for sale of goods, when damages are not clear. Used when contract would be fair to enforce. COVER DAMAGES—difference between contract price and cover price. Can go for damages (not cover) which is difference between market price at time of breach and contract price. UCC 2-712 and 2-723

1. SPECIFIC PERFORMANCE—forces promisor to perform contract

2. INJUNCTION—prohibits promisor from breaching contract; requires contract to be performed.

3. BOTH ARE APPROPRIATE WHERE DAMAGES ARE SPECULATIVE.

4. Court presumes that when one seeks equitable remedy:
   a. Restrictions on land are bad. If contract is oppressive, it is bad due to unequal bargaining power and unfairness.
   b. If contract is unfair at time made, then it is unenforceable, but if it is unfair at time of enforcement, you can't because people can't be expected to anticipate unfairness.
   c. Some courts say that if contract becomes unfair at any point then contract is not good and won't be enforced.
   d. In order to get equity, you must come into court with clean hands.

C. TYPES OF DAMAGES

1. COMPENSATORY—makes innocent party whole; to compensate innocent party for their loss; can't compensate when you can't prove loss.

2. PUNITIVE—not available for breach; contract law does not try to punish.

3. NOMINAL—awarded when there has in fact been a breach, but the promisee's damage is so small as to be incalculable. Acknowledges breach.

JOBS, INTERVIEWS, AND RESUMES

FINDING YOUR FIRST JOB

If you choose not to work during the summer after your first year of law school, you should try to find a legal position during your second year or the summer after your second year. Such positions serve various purposes. Since you may not know what kind of law you wish to practice, your first job may expose you to at least one area and help you narrow down your options. You will learn more about what you like, dislike, and look for in a permanent position. Clerking part-time also provides important practice in legal research and writing, and this experience should help your classroom performance.

In addition, your first job may provide you with a reference from an attorney, and references are obviously helpful when seeking full-time employment. Moreover, you may even be hired by the firm you work for since firms like to hire people they know and trust.

The Fall Recruiting Season: Where Did all The Suits Come From?

By the fall semester many students have changed their focus from classes and grades to jobs. Recruitment programs run by the school's placement office occur on campus each fall; and the hallways may resemble a zoo at this time. Everyone wants one of these high-paying summer associate positions, but only a few will get them. Don't fret, and keep your perspective. Such jobs represent only 17 percent of the job market; in other words, this is not the way most people find work.

The large law firms who offer these summer positions usually only interview the top students (usually the top 10-20 percent) at each school. Recruitment begins with on-campus interviews, which last from twenty to thirty minutes. At this stage the interviewer decides whether or not to invite the student back to the firm for a more complete interview, which may last for up to a day. Recruitment methods may include dinner parties, lunches, or other outings with members of the firm. As we said, however, the vast majority of students don't get a job through this overblown program. Most students find jobs through networking; that is, by getting involved with various legal groups and activities, and by making their connections through these.

Off-campus Job Searches

Smaller law firms do not come to campuses to interview. You have to approach them and persistently express your interest in being hired. The recruiting process tends to be much less lavish; smaller firms do not wine and dine potential clerks and/or associates.

In order to obtain a position with a smaller firm you should review the many job listings posted by the school placement or career services office, scour the classified ads, and conduct mass mailings. Many firms tend to hire alumni from the schools already represented in the firm, so a listing placed with a particular school generally means the firm is interested in hiring from that school. The career services or placement office also has lists of law firms, government agencies, and corporations you can approach even if they are not currently advertising positions.

Another possibility is to use free on-line legal computer services which have job searching capabilities, such as LEXIS and Westlaw. These resources can be used to generate mass mailings. Remember, however, that the response rate to mass mailings is often quite low. At best, a small percentage of your letters will lead to an interview.

Jobs Outside the Law Firm

Some of the more interesting and rewarding job opportunities are found outside law firms. Such jobs include judicial clerkships, and those with public interest law organizations, government departments, and legal research services. Working on legal publications is another possibility. Pursuing these career options will require independent effort on your part, since these organizations often do not come to schools or otherwise actively look for future employees.

And always remember: the reality of the job search process is that many jobs are obtained through friends, connections, or coincidences independent of your grades in law school.

Networking: It's a Who-You-Know World

Networking means making and maintaining contacts for mutual gain. It is only negative if done with duplicity, and that should not be the case. The aim of networking is to provide you with the best opportunity to obtain a law job, and the people you contact will probably have been there themselves. Many law school student organizations form "mentoring" programs, which pair students with alumni local attorneys as a networking device.

Your list of contacts will probably fall into the following groups:

- People and companies you know who could employ you

- People who can give you good advice, job leads, or the names of people who might be interested in hiring you

- Prominent people in your community

- Friends of your parents or anyone they know in the legal community

DEVELOPING AND WRITING A RESUME

Why Have an Outstanding Resume?

A good resume plays an important role in obtaining a job, and poor resumes cause prospective employers to view you negatively. You must make the best first impression you can on prospective employers; a resume is a self-advertisement designed to persuade these people that you are the best person for the job.

Your resume is the summary of your accomplishments in law school and your work experiences so far. It is obviously helpful to have valuable and distinguished credentials on your resume. The decisions you make regarding extracurricular activities, as well as your grades and class rank, should all be included. Thus, as you go through law school, you should keep your resume in mind as you commit to various activities.

Putting Your Best Foot Forward

Many people who have the credentials and positive qualities sought by employers have difficulty expressing this information effectively. Employers receive thousands of resumes each year, and will likely spend no more than a few moments reviewing yours. Therefore, your resume must be appealing to the eye, easy to read, and must contain the type of information the employer wants to know; it must convey a professional image.

Simplicity is often the key to organizing a visually effective resume. Look at your resume as if you are an employer who has already read dozens of them. Make sure you have adequate margins, plenty of blank space between entries, and logical organization. Your resume should also include the appropriate use of boldface type, underlining, and italics for emphasis.

In writing your resume use concise, active language. Verbs such as created, developed, demonstrated, organized, directed, evaluated, drafted, trained, and proposed are all powerful, active words. Avoid passive language like "was asked to. . ." or "was responsible for . . . ." Your responsibilities may be clear enough, but how you choose to present them can make all the difference.

A resume should be as long as necessary to present the most important facts about you. Don't leave out anything that highlights your skills and abilities. A one-page resume is preferred, but use two pages if you really need to.

How to Create a Resume

Create your resume by first writing down on a piece of paper everything you can think of about yourself and your accomplishments. Include honors, awards, and major achievements, as well as volunteer work, community service, and even those unglamorous summer jobs flipping burgers or waiting on tables. Describe your educational background, special talents, and interests. Think about your background as the interviewer does: What emphasizes your achievements, motivation, goal orientation, intellect, communication skills, and responsible work habits? Try to summarize this information in a way that best presents you.

There are a number of basic resume formats:

- The time-line or chronological resume
- The functional or skill resume
- The combination resume

The Time-line or Chronological Resume

The time-line or chronological resume is the most common resume style. It lists experiences in the order in which they occurred, with the most recent experience normally listed first. However, there are two potential problems with organizing your resume chronologically. First, it is difficult to account for empty time, such as the years you may have taken off between college and law school. Second, it is difficult to emphasize any particular skills or abilities, since the structure of the resume focuses on time and not skill.

The Functional or Skill Resume

The functional or skill resume, by contrast, highlights competencies, talents, and skills. Infomation is divided into categories under headings that are relevant to specific fields, such as law. Under each heading are summarized the experiences which support the existence of that skill or competency. These resumes downplay dates; however, they tend to be less clear than chronological resumes. For this reason, employers generally do not favor them.

The Combination Resume

The combination resume borrows from both of the above formats. The bulk of the information is presented chronologically, and is supplemented by one or two functional categories. The combination resume enables the writer to emphasize particular skills while presenting information in the preferred chronological order.

The combination format categorizes your experiences into sections, such as Education, Employment, and References. Under each heading, entries are listed in reverse chronological order, that is, beginning with the most recent experience. Each entry contains information on where you were, what you accomplished, and the length of time you were there. Begin each entry with the most impressive information so that weaker points are less prominent. If a lesser point is really insignificant, leave it out entirely.

The Structure of a Well-written Resume

A well-written resume should have your name, address, and contact number(s) at the top. Some resumes show both a local and permanent address (in cases where students are attending school away from their permanent home). This may be useful when you are job hunting outside your home area and seek to demonstrate contacts with another community or location. Remember to organize your resume by headings which subdivide the information about yourself into relevant parts. Typical headings are Education, Work Experience, Activities, Publications, and References, usually in that order.

List the educational institutions you have attended. Assuming that you are currently studying at a law school, that school will be the first one listed. Next, list the name of any school you attended for other graduate study, then the name of the school from which you received your undergraduate degree. This order is preferred by interviewers because they most often want to know where you are studying now.

Interviewers are often interested in learning about any academic honors you received, including scholarships, awards, honor society memberships, and placement on the Dean's List. Do not be modest. If you were awarded an honor, say so.

Extracurricular activities are also important, particularly if they involve the development of law-related skills such as oral advocacy or writing, or commitment to particular areas of the law, such as membership in a labor law society or as a contributor to a legal publication. A published paper in a legal journal should be cited completely on your resume. Such credentials remain important long after graduation and indicate your understanding of legal writing and citation. If you don't qualify for participation on the school law journal, you can still obtain a similar credential through successful applications to inter-school publications, professional journals, or national writing competitions.

The next category will be your experience and employment. Listing past experience reveals your skills and responsibilities. For each position indicate the law-related skills you learned, such as writing and speaking. Many people distinguish between "Legal," "Law-Related," and "Other Employment" in subheadings, enabling them to include a wide range of work. Legal jobs, clinical experiences, internships, research assistantships, and other non-legal but relevant work experience should all be included.

Experience in the legal field is naturally of particular interest to employers and is almost as important as your academic performance when it comes to interviews. Consequently, you should try to get as much law-related experience as you can while you are in school, if not before. You should also of course be careful to maintain good relationships with your past employers because you may want to use them as references.

In addition, include special skills which distinguish you from other candidates. Language fluency, computer experience, licenses, or certificates will all serve to differentiate you from others who have similar grades and class rank.

Some people wonder whether they should include personal information, such as health condition or date and place of birth, on their resume. As a rule, this information is not relevant and so should not be included. Likewise, information about your marital status, or politics and religion are not appropriate areas for inquiry.

Listing references is optional, but doing so will usually enhance your credibility. Do not include references until you have received their permission to do so. Also, advise them that they might be contacted. References included on your resume should be from people who can attest to your specific abilities. As with letters of recommendation, references from important people carry little weight if those people have no first-hand experience of your skills. For example, if the governor is a great friend of your mother, you are better advised to ask the governor to introduce you to individuals than to list him or her as a reference on your resume. If you decide not to specify references on your resume, then indicate that this information will be provided on request.

Writing samples and transcripts are also optional. Be prepared to provide either or both if an employer asks, and count on the employer reading them. A writing sample is something you can develop in a writing class, at work as a law clerk, or in preparation for a competition or law journal. It is writing that should not have been edited by someone other than yourself; that is, it must be your own work. Select a writing sample that is somewhat interesting in substance, in proper legal form, and has been proofread to detect any errors.

Potential employers may also ask for a copy of your law school transcript. Transcripts are useful to employers who wish to evaluate your overall performance during law school, and who want to know what courses were of interest to you. Transcripts may also be used to verify any academic-related claims; a copy should be available during all interviews, as should an explanation for any discrepancy or concern which a transcript may evidence.

To Include or Exclude?

Many students wonder whether grades should always be included. Whatever you decide, you should choose the route which best presents your strengths and does not highlight your weaknesses. Your law school G.P.A. may or may not be the best means of demonstrating your intelligence and capability to an employer.

As a guide, law school grades below a "B" are probably best omitted. Likewise, include class rank if it is positive information (upper one-third or better). If you don't indicate a grade point average on your resume, most people will assume that your grades are not worth extolling.

There are alternatives to simply stating your overall G.P.A. If your overall average is low but you have done well in a particular course concentration, consider showing your grades only in that area. In general, be creative about showing your intellect. Remember, 90 percent of those who successfully graduated from law school did not graduate in the top 10 percent of their classes.

Another point worth noting is that there is no rule against creating more than one resume. You may want a general resume and a tax-oriented resume, for example. This is perfectly acceptable and even recommended if you are looking for a job in a particular market.

A Sample Resume

The following outline illustrates the resume structure described above:

Contact Information

Name

Address

Telephone number

Education

List in reverse chronological order, starting with current law school; date when J.D. is expected; any honors and activities.

Then include any colleges attended, listing major and graduation date and any honors and activities.

Special certificates would also be included in this section of your resume.

Experience

List the name of the organization, its location, your position, responsibilities, and dates you worked there. If your title is a better indicator of the amount of responsibility than the name of the employer, list the title first, but do so with consistency. Avoid the use of the word "I" and use action words.

Employment

This section can include paid employment, volunteer work, internships, and summer jobs, provided you make the distinction between what was uncompensated employment/experience and what was not.

References

Will be provided on request.

Optional Resume Categories

Clinical Experience

Community Activities

Languages

Professional Affiliations

Publications

Special Skills

Intersets

THE COVER LETTER

Your resume should always be accompanied by a cover letter. The purpose of a cover letter is to introduce you to the prospective employer and set forth your intentions. For example: "I am writing in response to your job notice with our Office of Career Services" or "I am writing because I am interested in environmental law, and your firm is among the leaders in the field." The cover letter also gives you an opportunity to expand on the "general" information in your resume and to tie it specifically to the particular job for which you are applying.

The Significance of the Cover Letter

A well-written cover letter fills in the outline drawn by your resume and gives the employer a sense of your personality, enthusiasm, and level of organizational skills. A dull, poorly written, or insincere cover letter will probably be your first and last contact with the employer who receives it. Try to put yourself in the employer's place; he has had to slough through hundreds or thousands of letters and resumes before getting to yours. Make it interesting and to the point, and highlight the qualities the employer seeks.

The Key to an Effective Cover Letter

Make your cover letter as personal as possible: at the very least, the letter should be addressed to a particular person. Learn as much as you can about the firm you are applying for employment at before you sit down to write the letter. The information you gather will enable you to demonstrate in your letter that the decision to write that specific employer was an informed one, and was not simply inspired by the presence of the employer's name on a placement office's list.

If you do not know the name of the hiring partner or recruiting coordinator, telephone the employer and ask. Consider addressing your letter to someone in the firm who practices in your specialty area, or a graduate of your own school—in other words, someone who is likely to take some interest in your resume. If you can't track down a specific name and title, try harder. Still no luck? Then address the letter to the Chairperson, Recruitment Coordinator, or Hiring Committee, and use Dear Sir or Madam as the salutation.

End your cover letter by reminding the reader of your interest in and availability for an interview. If you plan to be traveling to the areas where the firms you are applying to are located, write them well in advance to arrange for a personal interview.

Your cover letter should be organized in the following way:

Introductory Paragraph

After the salutation, specify who you are (a second-year law student, for example), why you are writing, the position for which you are applying (associate, staff attorney, summer clerk, intern), and, if applicable, how you heard of the opening.

Second Paragraph

Explain why you are interested in working for the firm and describe what you have to offer in the way of training, credentials, experience, and special interests which would be appropriate to the practice or business involved.

Third Paragraph

Refer to the attached resume summarizing your qualifications. You may also give a summary or highlight of any other material you may be including (writing sample, transcript, reference list) or a description of your previous or present employment to illustrate your training, experience, and skills.

Concluding Paragraph

Indicate your availability for an interview, and offer to be available at the employer's convenience. Give your telephone number. Thank them for their consideration.

Following up the Initial Contact

Merely sending a cover letter with a resume does not guarantee that you will receive an immediate response. Indeed, many employers do not respond at all. Wait two or three weeks for a response to your first letter before following up with another letter or a telephone call.

Whether you are writing one letter or one hundred letters, keep track of each one—which ones were responded to, and which ones require following up. When you do not receive a response from an employer, you should contact the employer to find out your status. You should send follow-up letters when appropriate, thank employers for interviews, and inform employers of new academic developments (for exmaple, having made Law Review or a Moot Court team). Put effort into your cover letters; they reflect a lot about you and the kind of attorney you will be. Be fairly aggressive; employers are very busy and most will be impressed by your drive and enthusiasm.

INTERVIEWING

The Initial Interview

An initial interview at a law firm may be intimidating, but is likely to be relatively brief, an introductory meeting. It serves as a screening device to confirm your basic qualifications for the position. General appearance, required education, and appropriate work history are the main considerations in this short interview.

The Second Interview

A serious candidate will probably go through several interviews. The call-back interviews most often involve meeting several lawyers, touring the law firm's facilities, and possibly having lunch and dinner with members of the firm. Interviews with each attorney generally last from twenty to thirty minutes and aim to evaluate a candidate's knowledge, judgment, personality, fluency, and poise. Your answers to questions will usually not go unchallenged and will probably be followed up with more specific inquiries.

Interviewer Objectives

Remember that many interviewers have little experience at what they are doing; after all, they are attorneys, first and foremost. However, there are certain issues every interviewer has in mind when she sits down with an applicant. Be prepared to be asked why you wanted to become a lawyer, what your goals are, and why you are the best candidate for the job. Expect some of your interviewers to quiz you on legal issues to observe how you handle challenges. And be prepared to respond at moderate length to one of the most perplexing and frequently uttered sentences in the entire interview process: "So, tell me about yourself."

There are questions that you are not required to, and shouldn't, answer. For example, age, marital status, political affiliation, and religion are improper areas of inquiry. If a question concerning one or another of these issues is asked, point out, as politely and amiably as possible, that such questions are outside the scope of a hiring decision, which should be based on ability.

Successful Interviewing

Successful interviewing requires excellent communication skills. Most people cannot walk into an interview cold and be very effective. It takes practice to develop the ability to listen, respond, and think on your feet (or in your chair). While you are lucky in that the law school curriculum is designed to teach you such skills, adapting them to the special tension of the interview situation takes preparation and rehearsal. Making that effort will pay off in better job possibilities and personal satisfaction. Few feelings are as exhilarating as walking out of an interview knowing that it went well.

The interview may be more than important to your chances of securing employment at a particular firm—it may be decisive. A terrific interview can tip the scales for you even if your grades aren't the best or you are short on credentials. Use your personality to spark the interviewer's interest. Be aggressive and enthusiastic. Approach every interview as an opportunity for advancement, growth, and, at the very least, education.

If you feel that professional preparation might be helpful, ask your school's career guidance counselors for information about workshops or classes in interviewing. Courses in communication, debate, or oral advocacy may also contribute to your sense of security. When choosing a course, find out if the teacher will stage mock interviews in class. There is nothing like a thorough simulation to prepare for the real thing.

The importance of developing effective interview techniques cannot be stressed enough. Even the student who graduates near the top of her class is not guaranteed employment if she lacks the ability to communicate and interact effectively in an interview. But the process should not be looked upon with too much dread. The objectives of the interviewer and those of the interviewee are not so far apart. The applicant wants to get a sense of the firm's atmosphere and expectations, while the interviewer wants to evaluate the candidate's suitability for the position. The applicant wishes to convey his qualifications for employment; the interviewer wants the applicant to know the benefits and prestige the firm can offer. They are both trying to find out whether the applicant and the firm are right for each other, so to speak.

The Value of Preparation

If a candidate asks about the nature of the firm's practice, how many lawyers are in the firm, or other similarly basic questions, it is a sign he did not do his homework. It is not a good idea to appear unprepared. Lawyers tend to consider it a bad omen, since the majority of lawyering consists of preparation. The firm will have little concrete knowledge of the candidate to go by even at the time the hiring decision is made, so any absence of preparation may doom the applicant's standing.

So, learn about the firm by doing research and uncovering its history and the nature of the law its lawyers have practiced. In addition, think about questions you would like to ask the employer, such as whether there is flexibility in your potential area of practice.

Answering Questions

Think in advance about how you would respond to difficult questions. These may include inquiries about low grades or perhaps a lack of experience. Take time to consider your strengths and shortcomings honestly. Frank, undefensive answers to difficult questions require thought and analysis. There is too much at stake in these interviews to "wing it."

Answer closed or leading questions briefly, (e.g., "So, you lived at the Story Hall dormitory, I see?"), and open questions more completely (e.g., "Why did you major in mathematics in college?"). Remember, the interviewer has your resume in front of him. Try to add qualitative information that could not be expressed in your resume.

Here are a few sample interview questions with suggestions on how to answer them. Consider how you would want to respond to these or similar inquiries.

Questions About Work

Why do you want to work for this firm?
Show the interviewer you've given it some thought and you aren't just applying everywhere.

Are you willing to relocate? Are you set on what practice area you want?
Tell the interviewer if you have any concerns about moving to other parts of the country or reservations about a particular practice area. Be honest, but also bear in mind that the more limitations you place on the conditions of your employment, the less likely you are to get the job. Firms usually value flexibility.

What did you learn from your last job?
The interviewer wants to get a sense of your work ethic. Be more specific than, "I learned to work with people." This is too common a response. So is "I did some simple drafting and it really helped

me better understand the basics of the legal process." Rather, you might respond with something like, "I worked on a multi-million-dollar takeover offer researching a particular securities question under the recent change in the law."

How does this firm compare to others with whom you are interviewing?
If you want the job, find the ways in which the firm compares favorably. The key point here is not to fear admitting that you are interviewing with other firms. This makes you a more desirable applicant since it suggests that other firms are interested in your talents.

Questions About School
What courses did you enjoy the most? The least?
Whatever favorite courses you pick, be sure you can describe how they are significant in the context of the position for which you are interviewing. Try something like, "I liked Contracts the best. I know Contracts doesn't relate directly to arguing cases in court, but it helped me understand the language of the law better and taught me how to argue about an ambiguity. I also improved my writing abilities through writing exercises in class. I believe these skills are essential." With luck the courses you disliked will be unrelated to the job. You might have found those courses less interesting, but you should not indicate that they were too hard or too much work. Remember, the employer is always thinking about your ability to perform well regardless of what assignments are given to you.

Nonverbal Cues

Pay careful attention to nonverbal communication during the interview. These factors are as important as the substance of what is exchanged. In fact, nonverbal cues often convey the truth behind our words. Be aware of your body language and your manner of speaking and presentation.

Present an open appearance: keep your arms uncrossed and your expression pleasant. Don't be defensive: avoid folding your arms, leaning away, crossing your legs, or squinting as if you're trying too hard to concentrate on what is being said. Don't appear too judgmental by, for instance, striking a pose with your hand to your cheek, stroking your chin, or cocking your head slightly to one side. Sit up straight. Gesture moderately with your hands, but keep in mind that no gesture has just one meaning. Body language, just like spoken language, can be ambiguous and, therefore, must be precise and appropriate to the comment it's emphasizing.

Considerations for the Interviewee

Always remember that you are not the only one being evaluated. You, too, should have some judgments to make and questions to ask. Try to develop a sense of the law firm's general character, its atmosphere, and mode of operation. What is expected of new associates? Is there a rotation process? Can new associates bring in clients? To whom do new associates report? How long does it take to become a partner? Does the firm do pro bono work? Will the firm expand in the next several years? Learn what kinds of continuing training is provided for associates. Ask whether the firm encourages community involvement. Note that you do not have to ask each of these questions or even any of them directly in the interview, but you should keep these issues in mind as the interview progresses. Your primary goal is to get an offer of employment; there will be time after that to ask additional questions.

Afterword

That is what law school looks like from the inside out. We hope that you now have the confidence to get started down this road, knowing, before you start, that there is light at the end of the tunnel. The law is a fascinating, grueling, unparalleled discipline. It will seem opaque, labyrinthine, uncompromising; keep believing in yourself, follow the tips and suggestions in this book, and you can't help but succeed.

There are those who would argue that the world already has too many lawyers. It is a sad fact, however, that not everyone emerges from law school as motivated, talented, or well-qualified as you will. The world can never have too many eager, enthusiastic lawyers determined to serve their clients with tireless dedication.

You *can* get through law school. Tens of thousands of people do it every year. Only a few of those people have any natural talent for the task. Most approach it with nothing more than you have: curiosity, determination, and a stalwart belief in their own abilities.

So tackle your legal career with integrity and commitment and the rewards of the profession will come to you. We're confident that you will be one of the great ones. See you in court.

About the Authors

Paul M. Lisnek is the Director of Academics and Faculty of the National Institute for Legal Education. He is a nationally respected continuing legal education lecturer, jury expert, trial consultant, and the author of six other books. The former Assistant Dean of Loyola University of Chicago School of Law, Dr. Lisnek has also taught at the University of Illinois at Urbana, DePaul University at Chicago, and Pepperdine University Law School. His law degree and Ph.D. were earned at the University of Illinois. He has been appointed by the Illinois Supreme Court as a Commissioner and Inquiry Panel Chairperson of the Illinois Attorney Registration and Disciplinary Commission. Dr. Lisnek is the former president of the American Society of Trial Consultants and also serves as a legal and jury expert for NBC News, appearing regularly on the *Today Show, Weekend Today,* and the *Nightly News with Tom Brokaw,* among other television and radio programs.

Steven I. Friedland is a visiting professor at Georgia State University School of Law. He graduated with honors from Harvard Law School, where he was Senior Editor of the Harvard Law Record and Editor of the Harvard Environmental Law Review. Professor Friedland has served as an Assistant United States Attorney in Washington, D.C., and taught at American University School of Justice, University of Miami Law School, and Nova Southeastern University Law Center. He holds an LLM from Columbia Law School, is currently in the SJD program there, and is the author of several books and articles. Professor Friedland was a Dollard Fellow in Law, Medicine, and

Psychiatry at Columbia Medical School in 1993, and has won teaching awards at several schools. He has served as a faculty member of the National Institute for Legal Education for the last six years.

Chris M. Salamone is the founder and Executive Director of the National Institute for Legal Education. He is also the founder and chairperson of the National Law and Leadership Foundation, a non-profit organization dedicated to developing values and leadership potential in America's youth. Mr. Salamone is a senior partner with the law firm of Salamone & Mosca, based in Boca Raton, Florida, where he represents high profile clients and serves as General Counsel to several national corporations. He graduated third in his law school class, receiving magna cum laude and Law Review honors. He is a member of the teaching faculty of the National Institute of Trial Advocacy and has served on the Judicial Nominating and Tenure Committee. Mr. Salamone is a frequent lecturer on legal issues, and is a member of both the Florida and New Jersey bars.